A Sense of the Divine

A Sense of the Divine
The Natural Environment
from a Theocentric Perspective

James M. Gustafson

The Pilgrim Press
Cleveland, Ohio

The Pilgrim Press, Cleveland, Ohio 44115
© 1994 by Baldwin-Wallace College
Paperback edition 1996

Printed in the United States of America on acid-free paper

99   98   97   96   5   4   3   2   1

Library of Congress Cataloging-in-Publication Data

Gustafson, James M.
A sense of the divine : the natural environment from a
theocentric perspective / James M. Gustafson.
p.   cm.
Includes bibliographical references and index.
ISBN 0-8298-1003-X (cloth : acid-free paper)
ISBN 0-8298-1100-1 (paperback : acid-free paper)
1. Nature—Religious aspects—Christianity.
2. Human ecology—Religious aspects—Christianity.
3. Environmental ethics.   4. Christian ethics.   I. Title.
BT695.5.G87   1994
241′.691—dc20
94-3890
CIP

Contents

Foreword

Moll Professor of Faith and Life
Baldwin-Wallace College

Because we live in an age of strident voices, it is not our habit to be attentive, to listen on tiptoe rather than casually overhear, to acknowledge and heed rather than absentmindedly entertain. Careful consideration of ethical issues requires deliberate and attentive reciprocity, but in an age of shouting matches, earnest dialogue conducted in precise terms becomes a lost whisper amid the noise of diatribes and campaigns of moral conquest. Doves and hawks alike, pro-life and pro-choice partisans, deep ecologists, animal liberationists, millennialists and absolutists of every stripe imaginable shout instructions to everyone in earshot, callous to how the audience is faring and oblivious to what dissenters might contribute to the discussion. Strident voices do not echo diversity or ameliorate moral ambiguities. Today we are berated by howling evangelists on crusades who are convinced that a moral life demands unequivocal action of a prescribed sort. Ethics is reduced to catechism. Because we live in a age of moral evangelism, bludgeoned by strident cries at every turn, it is not our habit to be attentive, to heed, to acknowledge, to listen intensely as we venture to speak to the problems of our time. As a result we ignore what is at stake for others. Were we to write books about ethics and the environment, we would surely be tempted simply to take sides and join the shouting match.

In such an age of competing dogmatism, it is refreshing to hear an authentic call to ethical responsibility, clearly expressed in a musical voice, modest yet emphatic and without euphemistic contamination. There are no answers in the back of this book. No reprieve from ambiguity and risk is offered. We are never let off the hook. The purpose of the book is not to direct moral traffic. It is to call us into a broadened moral consciousness, to awaken us to the legitimate claims and stakes of all who participate in the world of nature. The ethical dilemmas we face in the dissonance and coherence of nature and the environment are not to be lamented any more than life itself. They offer our only opportunities to become responsible citizens in nature.

The Moll Lectures delivered by James Gustafson provided the Baldwin-Wallace College community a welcome reprieve from the shrillness of much contemporary debate. Historically this series has served as a bridge between the academy and the church, offering an exchange of views rather than didactic pronouncements. To preface his lectures, Professor Gustafson conducted a seminar for students on ethical issues in the presidential election and a workshop for faculty who are attempting to incorporate ethics appropriately into a liberal arts curriculum. I report this because I want to introduce the voice you will hear speaking in these pages rather than preface what he says. Gustafson addresses his readers personally and individually even as he discusses the ambiguities of shared identity and existence. When most accusing, his voice remains that of a friend. Readers who have been offered the friendship of a great mind are appropriately advised to give their careful attention.

Some readers will be disappointed to learn that if they are to become truly responsible amid the ambiguities of nature, they must continually risk acting without the benefit of prior certainty concerning the fitness of their choices. But surely there will be others who are overcome with gratitude for being gently but unequivocally reminded that ethical responsibility is first and without ceasing their *very own response—*

indeed, the *je einige* response of the attentive who are perpetually engaged by the voices of alien species and strangers speaking in foreign tongues who evoke responsibility in the midst of ambiguity. Ethical responsibility is the venture one makes as one risks being wrong in order to do what is perhaps right. The character of ethical behavior consists largely in the manner of address and response.

Before we can address the problems of the environment, we must first be addressed ourselves. We must first hear the live voices of diverse neighbors, wondrous creatures great and small. We must hear something more than the echo of our own thoughts, "our own love back in copy speech," as Robert Frost wrote. Yet, even live voices are seldom engaging when merely overheard. We rarely hear, much less heed, what is addressed to someone else. Yet conversely, to know ourselves as addressed can awaken us from dogmatic slumber and present us with "counter-love, original response." Even the alien voice of a stranger speaking in a foreign tongue—perhaps especially that voice—can enlighten the dark night of moral loneliness and perpetual ambiguity by evoking the courage to risk responsibility. Responding to the uninvited voices of what is foreign to us, we finally venture to participate actively in the ambiguous world of nature. My advice to those pondering this book is to listen attentively until engaged by these lectures rather than simply to read them. Respond to Gustafson in lively dialogue. Expect to be addressed. Allow his voice to reverberate in your imagination. The same sentences revisited will surely speak with expanded meaning and new significance.

These lectures seem haunted by a primal moral urge, growing, Gustafson suggests, from that primal experience of revulsion which Hans Jonas observed precedes all thought about what is good or any notion of what is at stake in shared existence. Evil *is* more vivid than good, and a prior revulsion does prompt whatever images we frame of the good. There is, then, at least this possibility for those who seek some universal quality or common denominator within the dissonance and ambiguity experienced in nature. We should remember, however, that genuine contributions to the discussion of ethics and the environment are not made by revealing some hidden coherence within nature (discovering the universal solvent!) in order to orchestrate the behavior of others. Neither are genuine contributions expressed in the shrill voices so often heard in this age of partisan dogmatism. Liberating contributions are made rather by the musical voices of those who gain and share the most coherent interpretation they can of nature and human existence in a shared environment. Such a voice resounds in the pages that follow.

Reference

The quotations are from Robert Frost, "The Most of It," in *Complete Poems of Robert Frost* (New York: Holt, Rinehart & Winston, 1964), 451.

Preface

The Moll Lectures delivered at Baldwin-Wallace College in November 1992 provided the occasion for me to reflect more specifically upon issues to which only allusions are made in *Ethics from a Theocentric Perspective,* and supplement the four chapters of the second volume which address particular arenas of human activity. The natural environment was clearly in my consciousness throughout the writing of both volumes, but I chose not to isolate it for special attention in the illustrative sections of the second volume. Publications about ecological ethics, attitudes toward nature, and so on, were burgeoning at the time I wrote *Ethics from a Theocentric Perspective,* and the rate of increase has been almost astronomical since then. Given all that I have read and material I have not studied, would there be anything distinctive to say about the topic? If there is, it has to show that the theocentric perspective from which I developed ethics makes some difference in the way we think and act. "Some difference" is all that can be claimed, and not a decisive difference in many aspects of the interpretation of the natural environment.

The lecture audience of students, clergy, faculty members, and other interested persons affected two aspects of this book. First, I have reviewed in a general way a number of alternative perspectives to set my own in their context. To some readers, perhaps many, much of this is redundant. Second, I have not engaged in technical argument in technical terms and have resorted to an old habit of using very commonplace experiences and observations about them to lead into more general matters. The four illustrative chapters of the second volume of *Ethics from a Theocentric Perspective* follow hundreds of pages of delineation and defense of the theocentric perspective. It cannot be assumed that readers of the Moll Lectures are acquainted with all that, and thus I have drawn attention in this book to the major aspects of the perspective without developing its defense.

The lectures as delivered have been expanded here. Some material that was barely outlined has been filled out, and I have drawn from materials prepared for other purposes in doing so. These are noted in the acknowledgments that follow. My studying, since assuming the Luce Professorship at Emory University, has been very diverse because the books used in the Luce Faculty Seminar are selected in consultation with participants from different disciplines and professional schools. All three of the themes used in the first four years of that program have relevance to the Moll Lectures, "Human Being and Being Human," which brought explanatory sciences of the human into interaction with humanistic accounts, the idea of responsibility, and the idea of nature. What I have learned in preparation for those seminars and from my privileged position of conducting them, that is, from my faculty colleagues, is represented more by allusions than by specific attention in this book. Ethics and theology have not been the primary focus of attention in the Luce Seminars, but just as other participants reflect on the significance of materials and methodologies of other disciplines than their own for their teaching and research, so I ponder the importance of them for what has been my primary occupation for forty years.

The increments of understanding of the natural environment in this book are modest. I hope it provides readable access to alternative approaches as well as insight into how a theocentric perspective provides an understanding and interpretation of the natural world.

Reference

Persons interested in the previous work of which this is another illustration can see James M. Gustafson, *Ethics from a Theocentric Perspective*, 2 vols. (Chicago: University of Chicago Press, 1981 and 1984).

Acknowledgments

I am grateful to Baldwin-Wallace College for the invitation to deliver the Moll Lectures, and particularly to Professor Frederick Blumer, who holds the Theo and Belle Moll Chair in Faith and Life, and Professor David Krueger, who holds the Charles E. Spahr Chair in Managerial and Corporate Ethics. Their confidence in my ability to speak on a much-discussed topic, their personal hospitality, and the pleasant arrangements made for my wife and me all made our visit especially memorable. *The Christian Century,* also a sponsor of the lectures, brought attention to them from pastors and others; thus the audiences were appropriately faculty, students, pastors, and others interested in the topic. A long and vigorous session with more than twenty faculty members before the first lecture provided an opportunity to engage their thinking and to demonstrate in a brief way what the Luce Faculty Seminar I conduct at Emory does. Professor Michael Melampy, from the biology department, and David Krueger responded to the lectures with great care and incisiveness.

Chapter 4 is an expansion of material that was in the second lecture and a revision of a paper prepared for the U.S. Information Service for an Intercultural Symposium held in Chiang Mai, Thailand, in June 1990— one of the best-prepared and most vigorously conducted events in which I have participated. Bill McKibben and Donald Swearer were particularly important to me, among American participants.

Many authors and books are cited or alluded to; two that especially energized my preparation of the Moll Lectures were James Nash's *Loving Creation* and Jessica Tuchman Mathews's edited volume, *Preserving the Global Environment.*

These lectures and everything I write now are in overt and mysterious ways affected by my colleagues at Emory who participate in the Luce Faculty Seminar. My intensive exposure to representative writings from various disciplines and professional schools, and to scholar-teachers who are much more familiar than I with each of them, has significantly shifted my point of departure on any intellectual journey I now undertake, even if it travels to and through the familiar territory of my earlier career.

Sylvia Johnson Everett has competently, patiently, and interestingly not only overcome my technological retardation, but also provided a colleagueship in which to make the three Moll Lectures into this book.

Introduction

Our human experiences of the natural environment vary with the particular ways in which we are engaged in it: with decisive personal experiences that have affected our attitudes and outlooks; with the modes of explanation we have learned to apply to it; with the spheres (everywhere from the cosmos to our gardens) to which we attend; with the extent to which we are directly susceptible to its vicissitudes—threatening or sustaining our livelihoods; with moral and religious ideas and passions that direct our responses to it; and with the groups and institutions, policies and practices we have adopted in relation to it.

Some personal memoirs will serve to explain my own engagement with the natural environment. I grew up with a father who spent the first sixteen years of his life in the far north of Sweden. His father worked on the construction of the railroads as they moved north, and each child was born in a different place as the work progressed to the terminus of the rail system in the iron ore region of Swedish Lapland and its extension to Narvik, Norway, where the harbor never froze as it did in Luleå on the Gulf of Bothnia. During 1898–1899, his father also worked on the first power dam on the Ume River, now a state museum, and my father worked as a tool carrier on that project when he was nine. While technology and industrial interests were penetrating what was almost wilderness, my father, like almost all Swedes I have known well, retained a deep respect for the natural environment and an almost mystical relation to waterfalls, birch trees, and other of its aspects. (I once met the Swedish immigrant theologian Nels F. S. Ferré, whom I knew from biographical data was born in Luleå where my father's family finally settled. When I told him my father was also a "Luleåbo," his first response was, "The birch trees are so beautiful in Luleå." What is it about birches for many Northern Europeans? One notes a special love for them also in some Russian literature.)

My boyhood was spent on the Upper Peninsula of Michigan, which my father always called "God's Country." It was, like inland Maine and a few other places, as much like his home as one could find in the United States. Many of my experiences there helped form my devotion to and respect for the natural environment: walking in the woods and along the "piers" of the Menomonee River on the Michigan-Wisconsin border; learning at a very early age to identify different pine trees both by bark and by needles; noticing and naming different ground covers; picking and chewing wintergreen leaves; picking wild raspberries, blueberries, and strawberries as well as hazelnuts; respecting the arbutus, which we recognized as an endangered species of early spring flower before that term was common; being upset by the pollution of the Menomonee River from the Kimberly-Clark paper mill in Niagara, Wisconsin, which ruined it for fishing below that town; fishing off a raft made from an old Coca-Cola sign floating on four empty barrels on Brown's Lake, arrived at over miles of logging roads that went through "Cat's Ass Canyon"; hearing the screams of drowning girls offshore at Hamilton Lake; caring for the elm trees my father had planted in front of the parsonage where we lived and around the adjacent church (they broke the monopoly of Norway maples on both sides of Brown Street); canoeing on Spread Eagle Lake; chopping and piling wood for the kitchen range; skiing, sledding, tobogganing, and ice skating through the winter months;

3

delivering the *Iron Mountain News* each late afternoon in temperatures that someties went to forty degrees below zero and through knee-deep snows; feeling disgust at the ugly slag heaps from the iron ore mine that sustained our town's economy until the Great Depression, the dangerous open pits on Norway Hill from earlier mines, and "Red Creek," which carried the pumped water from the mines and flowed into "White Creek," which was pure enough to drink from; knowing that livelihood for our town was dependent upon that mine, and on logging both for lumber and for paper; raising a three-quarter-acre field of green and wax beans one summer to earn twenty-six dollars to buy my first bicycle; and being devastated when out of necessity my father moved us from "God's Country" to a rural village in Kansas.

Nature's beauty brought peace and awe. We used its resources for our sustenance, recognizing both the harmful and beneficial outcomes of that. We knew its powers to harm and destroy and thus learned to adapt to its threats.

In Kansas I saw my first tornado and the outcomes of the sustained drought of the thirties. Later, on the Burma-China border during the Second World War, I relished the lushness of the jungle, the shimmering heat over the rice paddies in the Shweli River valley, the blending and contrasting shades of green from the bamboo clusters in which Shans had their villages up the foothills to the mountaintops, even during monsoon season when about twenty inches of rain fell in a week. The noises of animal and bird life, day and night there, like the barking of the jackal back in Assam and Bengal, I can still recall, as well as trying to tramp through ankle-deep mud to locate and repair the break in a ground telephone line along our portion of the Ledo Road.

One could say, I suppose, that my consciousness of nature was formed "pre-reflexively," without scientific or aesthetic theories to explain and justify how nature and we were mutually engaged, without ethical theories to support both the limits of our exploitation of nature and our uses of it. My father's pastoral prayers in Swedish began, almost monotonously, with "Dear God, our heavenly Father, we thank you for . . ." and always included the natural environment without worrying about whether he was a pantheist, a pan-psychist, or had a radically transcendent God. I recall vividly his concern for future generations, though he had no theory of obligation to them; he would wonder what would happen if coal resources were exhausted, if oil resources were depleted, if iron ore was all mined out. But I think it never occurred to him that the Lake Superior trout and whitefish—delicacies we gorged ourselves on when we rarely visited his sister who lived on that lake in Wisconsin and some of whose family fished commercially—would be threatened by changes in the ecology due to building the Saint Lawrence Seaway.

Some deep, but temporary, alteration of my human spirit still takes place when I arrive on the shore of Lake Au Train on the Upper Peninsula, its lovely falls above it; and below it, the many miles of shallow winding of its river into Lake Superior, only two or three miles to the north as the crow flies, or when my grandson and I canoe stealthily on Lake Androscoggin in Maine around the island that is home to eagles, blue herons, ospreys, and other wonderful birds, and especially when we can glide within a few feet of placidly floating loons. Hearing the cry of the loon there is for me, like many other persons who grew up in those northern climes, a powerful experience. To be sure, these are not the only places that deeply affect my spirit; the weeks spent occasionally over thirty years at the Ghost Ranch in northern New Mexico always had a similar effect, evoked by a radically different landscape.

But now the "pre-reflexive consciousness" is often disturbed by a reflexive consciousness—by more scientific knowledge, more detailed accounts of the effects of human participation in nature and especially by the developments of technologies, political and economic policy alternatives, various ecological theories and their different outcomes for ethical approaches. The sweet innocence, the joy of consenting to the given, is disturbed, and those moments of deep awe and overwhelming delight require a bracketing of the sophistication that has accrued. Too quickly, but also quite properly, one's consciousness moves from appreciation and receptivity to a range of problematics and concern for preservation, for the inexorable conflicts of values between ends of economic development and ends of sheer peace and joy. One wonders whether laws that prohibit building within one hundred feet of a shoreline are sufficient to keep a lake from being converted into extensive resorts, or if the fish one catches are carrying dangerous effects of acid rain. One's engagement with the natural environment is altered by a different consciousness: even one's viewing it, not to mention one's actions in it.

Other people have different experiences. In responding to a request for a brief article on "Earth" for the journal *The Living Pulpit,* I recalled four other distinctive engagements, and I incorporate them in this introduction.

"When we walked barefoot through the puddles in the driveway, it was nice to feel the mud between our toes." This sentence is from Ronald Jager's delightful memoirs of growing up on a Northern Michigan farm. (We "UPers" would always ask if that referred to the northern part of the Lower Peninsula or to the Upper Peninsula; Jager's "northern" was southern to us.) Feeling mud oozing up between toes is a pleasant, nonrational, sensuous, tactile experience of the natural environment. It evokes fond memories for my wife, who had similar experiences during barefooted summer days on a farm in Iowa. The feeling is really quite indescribable; one has to experience it to know it. And my wife's older sister, who was not a tomboy, probably found it disgusting. Maybe it is like Jonathan Edwards's query about how to describe the taste of honey; if one had never tasted it, one could not know it. I suppose that Jager and my wife from time to time inadvertently stepped on a thick plop of fresh cow dung that also oozed between the toes. Was the experience the same? Or did the aspect of nature that engaged one make a difference between enjoyment and disgust?

"As for the natural world, we must try to restore wonder there too. We could start with that photograph of the earth. . . . We are the first generation to have seen it, the last generation to take it for granted. Will we remember what it meant to us? How fine the earth looked, dangled in space? How pretty against the endless black? How round? How very breakable? How small?" These words were written by my good friend Melvin Konner, a bioanthropologist dedicated to the use of scientific methods to explain as comprehensively as possible the nature and action of human beings. But, after several hundred pages he is moved to reflect upon the impoverishing depletion of the sense of wonder that can be the effect of an exclusively scientific interpretation. Just as he says that we "must try again to experience the human soul as soul, and not just as a buzz of bioelectricity; the human will as will, and not just a surge of hormones; the human heart not as a fibrous, sticky pump, but as the metaphoric organ of understanding," so we must recall that memorable photograph of the earth taken from outer space, immortalized on a postage stamp among other places. Meditation on that picture evokes aesthetic and moral responses to the earth: it has beauty against the endless black; it is round, breakable, small. Our human lives and activity are set into a radically different context; our engagement with nature is dramatically different from feeling the mud ooze up between our toes. Konner's words and the photograph he calls us to remember do not require a philosophically sophisticated ethical theory to make

9

his point. We have a deeply affective experience of our globe, our place in the cosmos, that evokes both wonder and a sense of responsibility.

"The process by which the planet Earth prepared itself for life is called pre-biotic evolution. The study of pre-biotic evolution divides itself into three main stages which one may label with the names 'geophysical,' 'chemical' and 'biological.'" This quotation comes from Freeman Dyson's Gifford Lectures, *Infinite in All Directions.* The title of the chapter from which they are drawn is "Why Is Life So Complicated?" This brilliant physicist, who clearly has religious sensibilities and an audacious imagination, attempts to provide the best explanation possible of the origins and probable future of the whole universe, including the development of life on our planet and its probable destiny. Here the natural environment is cosmic, planetary, yet as local as the niche of my garden, and it includes you and me. The modes of explanation are comprehensive— cosmology, physics, chemistry, paleontology, biology, etc. They are knitted together to account for almost everything, though not really a "theory of everything." Dyson calls himself a Socinian in theology; he does not refrain from speculation about a deity, likely a kind of cosmic mind, nor about eschatology, likely an infinitely open universe that can be populated with life on the basis of his practical suggestions even when life on our planet is threatened with demise. Here we have something very different from feeling mud between our toes and from the sense of wonder to which Konner is led after an intensive effort to explain scientifically our human life and activity. Nature is something to be explained, though not without some sense of its mystery.

"So it was; God made wild animals, cattle, and all reptiles, each according to its kind; and God saw that it was good. . . . God saw all that God had made, and it was very good." These familiar words from the first creation account in Genesis express the ancient response of the sources of our own religious tradition to being human in the midst of nature that humans did not and cannot create—assurance of its goodness, thankfulness for its diversity. It is an experience of nature in the light of faith in God; God is invoked as the creator who saw that all that was made was very good. Mud through one's toes, planet Earth seen from outer space, geophysical, chemical, and biological processes all can be interpreted as signs of the goodness of creation and of the goodness of the Creator.

Each of these describes or interprets an experience of nature. The levels of generality of interpretation differ according to the scope of nature that is attended to.

The contemporary Thai Buddhist monk Bhikkhu

Buddhadāsa, who is very deeply concerned about the effects on the environment of Southeast Asia as a result of recent industrial, economic, and technological activity, believes that "nothing exists independently; everything exists *interdependently,*" and that "anything which exists in a proper condition is in equilibrium with everything else." The first part of the quotation is similar to what I and others affirm, what Edward Farley has called, with reference to my work, a "common sense ontology." The second part is more problematic; it introduces a norm of what the "proper condition" of each and everything is; it alleges an equilibrium of each with everything else.

Some of us find that assumption to be too static, too harmonious. And from the perspective of human experiences of nature we wonder about the status of volcanic eruptions that not only destroy economies and communities but spew ashes that can affect the weather all over the world; hurricanes that tear through populated areas leaving thousands homeless, hungry, and jobless; droughts that mercilessly wither crops needed for human survival, not to mention the economic, technological, political, and consumer factors that drastically alter the interdependencies that might once have been in equilibrium, or ideally ought to be. Disturbances are both "natural" and human, and the human disturbances are the outcomes of the "nature" of our humanity—our capacities to survive, to increase knowledge, to utilize what is given for both justifiable and dubious human ends.

We do not experience interdependence in the abstract; we experience it in more or less inclusive particularities. "God is in the details." I have seen this attributed to Mies van der Rohe and to Albert Einstein; whomever the originator of the comment, it is a profound and pregnant statement. Like nature—which can be as specific to our experience as mud or cow dung oozing between our toes, or as abstract as Dyson's theory of why life is so complex or as Stephen Hawking's proposals in A Brief History of Time—the reality of God, the power that brings life into being, is confronted in the fierceness of volcanic eruptions, in the delicacy of the blossom of a deciduous azalea tree, in the air of a spring day that even smells verdant, in the song of the towhee and the mockingbird. But God is also in the *ordering* of the details, sensed in that icon or cartoon of spiraled DNA, in the metaphysical speculations of Benedict de Spinoza or Alfred North Whitehead, in the narratives of the people of the Jewish Scriptures, and in the biological explanations of the illnesses that inevitably bring about our deaths. God is in the details, but God is also in the ordering of the details, from which generalizations can be made in the symbolic script of mathematics, the stories of the Bible, the concepts of the metaphysicians, the metaphoric expressions of the poets, the efforts of theologians to verbalize what it means to be *In the Face of Mystery.*

We meet God through nature, as well as through historical and interpersonal human events. We meet God as the power that brings all things into being, that bears down on them and threatens and limits them, that sustains them and is the condition of possibility for their change. But we do not meet that power in the abstract; we meet it in the details. We do not meet the threats and limits in general; we meet them in specifics. We do not meet the possibilities for change in metaphysical or theological theories; we meet them in the details to which aspects of nature and of our human nature react and respond. We *experience* the reality of the Divine. Not everyone calls it the Divine, and those of us who do are often criticized because our interpretation of the presence of the Divine in the details does not satisfy certain standards of traditional theology or get resolved in its logical problematics. These are not trivial matters, and discussion of their difficulties in my delineation of a theocentric perspective is amply present in the published critiques of my work. The critiques, which I have not satisfactorily resolved for those who make them, will not be dealt with in this small book. Rather, as various chapters are developed I attempt to show how my version of the theocentric perspective affects both our experience and our interpretation of the natural environment.

To speak about environmental ethics in a distinctive voice is difficult, if not impossible. Environmental ethics certainly competes with bioethics and business ethics in the market of what I have called "Ethics: An American Growth Industry." While each of the applied areas of ethics is enlarged from the focus of particular moral choices, environmental ethics expands far beyond the others. One can begin with an experimental medical therapy using the new genetics and move by steps to what constitutes the distinctive nature of the human—no little question—as Dr. French Anderson of the National Institutes of Health has done. One can read the arguments about the morality of abortion and quickly see that the controverted questions are grounded in fundamental issues: the status of fetal life as person, developing person, or nonperson; the focus on the fetus or the mother as the physician's primary patient; the rights of the unborn against the rights of a woman to determine her bodily activity; and differences in religious and moral traditions. One can begin with the care of the dying and be embroiled in debates over whether heroic procedures are extending life or delaying dying, whether a noncognitive state of a patient constitutes the value of being a person, whether cost-benefit ratios ought to count in the determinations of interventions, and whether technology has usurped the natural course of events in ways beyond moral and medical justification.

One can begin with something as frequent as a consumer's choice and move by steps to tax policies and international economics. One can examine the survival efforts of a bloated corporation such as General Motors and find that free market recommendations eliminate much consideration of the responsibilities to employees and their communities, that outsourcing to cheaper labor markets complicates international trade, that reorganization of structures of authority comes from pressures of shareholders more than from internal decisions, and that world economics is entwined with domestic and international politics. Or one can look at the addiction to the automobile in many parts of the world and see its impact upon urban land use, on the natural environment, on choices about expenditures by governments when roads compete with mass transit.

When we think about the environment we move at least to the whole of our planet, and in full-length treatment have to take account of medical, economic, political, legal and regulative, biological, and climatological processes, at least. How difficult it is to bring all these parts into a coherent whole can be seen by reading a recent book called *Ecology, Economics, Ethics: The Broken Circle.* While the circle is a bit less broken when the editors knit together the contributions of various authors, there are still gaps. I cannot promise to be more successful than those who have concentrated on the issues more intensively than I.

In these chapters I attend to areas that I find present in all efforts to be comprehensive, and interpret them in the light of my own thinking and previous publications. The first chapter examines "A Moral Stance" and asks, "Why are we concerned?" I look at some answers to that question and make a case that for many people there is at least an implicit sense of the sublime if not an explicit "sense of the divine" in nature that often underlies other reasons for our concern. A theocentric perspective provides one way to describe and understand this sense of the divine and in turn to elicit it more deeply and fully.

In the second chapter I focus on human accountability and the conflicts of purpose that lead inevitably to ambiguous moral choices, and perhaps in some cases to tragic ones. Moral ambiguity pervades medical and economic choices as well, but in ecological issues it has particular dimensions. Living with moral ambiguity is a fact of life as humans intervene in the natural world, and while it is the task of ethics to seek to reduce, if not eliminate it, our success is limited. The third chapter offers an ideal-typology of different stances of responsibility toward nature, with some discussion of the religious or theological correlates of each type, and makes a case for one type, humans as participants in nature, as appropriate to a theocentric perspective.

In the fourth chapter I focus more on some relevant academic disciplines, those that contribute to discussions and resolutions of environmental policy, and question whether the disciplinary arcs can be closed to form the circle described in the recent book I mentioned. In the final chapter I argue that persons responsible for choices, whether an individual consumer choice, a choice about locating factories or offices, a governmental choice about transportation policy, or a legal choice about the law of the sea, have to attempt to close the circle. Choices under conditions of limited circumstances weigh the various disciplines and their important contributions, but premature closure of the circle is likely to lead to policies and actions that are directed by limited values and interests. The parts seldom, if ever, come into a whole harmonious equilibrium that my Thai monk affirms to be the reality.

All through this book is a persistent problem both for thought and for feelings and loyalties, namely, how various aspects or parts are related to the larger whole that we acknowledge. In a sense, the text and anti-text of these lectures, the belief that is both attractive and inadequate for many reasons, can be taken from Bhikkhu Buddhadāsa. The text is, "It follows that the essence of nature is socialism; nothing can exist independently; everything exists interdependently." Whether one calls it socialism or not, I take the descriptive statement to be true. The monk's further inference is the problematic part; it is my anti-text: "Anything which exists in a proper condition is in equilibrium with everything else."

References and Bibliographical Notes

My article, "Interdependence and Responsibility," appears in *The Living Pulpit* 2, no. 2 (1993): 44–45. The Ronald Jager quotation is from *Eighty Acres: Elegy for a Family Farm* (Boston: Beacon Press, 1990), xii. Jonathan Edwards's discussion of the taste of honey is from *Religious Affections* (New Haven: Yale University Press, 1959), 208–9. Konner's reflections are from the end of *The Tangled Wing: Biological Constraints on the Human Spirit* (New York: Harper Colophon Books, 1982), 435 and 436. The quotation from Dyson begins the chapter cited in the text; *Infinite in All Directions* (New York: Harper and Row, 1988), 74. The New English Bible was used to quote Genesis 1:24–25. Donald K. Swearer is editor of *Me and Mine* (Albany: State University of New York Press, 1989), which is a selection of essays by Bhikkhu Buddhadāsa; the quotation is from page 165. Edward Farley's comments are from Harlan R. Beckley and Charles M. Swezey, eds., *James M. Gustafson's Theocentric Ethics* (Macon, Ga.: Mercer University Press, 1988), 40–42. Stephen Hawking's book, *A Brief History of Time*, was published in 1988 (New York: Bantam Books). I refer to Gordon Kaufman's magnum opus, *In the Face of Mystery* (Cambridge: Harvard University Press, 1993), in which he takes account of many items I have tried to and comes to very different conclusions about how we meaningfully talk about God. "Ethics: An American Growth Industry," was published in *The Key Reporter* 56, no. 3 (Spring 1991): 1–5. Dr. French Anderson's forthcoming paper, "Can We Alter Our Humanness by Genetic Engineering?" develops aspects of the human that can be altered and argues for this conclusion: "I believe that if there are uniquely human characteristics that are beyond our physical hardware, we simply cannot alter them." He tentatively supports the idea of "soul." F. Herbert Bormann and Stephen R. Kellert are editors of *Ecology, Economics, Ethics: The Broken Circle* (New Haven: Yale University Press, 1991), to which I refer at various points; Holmes Ralston III has an excellent chapter on ecological ethics.

1

The Sense of the Divine
A Moral Stance

Our stance toward the natural environment, whether it is one of exploitative utilization, mystical or aesthetic appreciation, rational discrimination of proper and improper human uses, or some combination of these and others, is evoked by some experiences of it. We never experience it as a whole; we experience aspects of it. As I indicated in the introduction, that might be mud oozing between one's toes, or the larger complications of life to be explained. Our stance is not unmediated; it is culturally affected by values we imbibe in our time and place, socialized by our families and religious outlooks, or focused by our consciousness of threats to well-being that occur, or by our indignant passions when we see and feel threats to it. Our experiences and our stances are usually correlated in a pre-reflexive way.

In 1956 my family and I drove from Ashland, Wisconsin, on the shore of Lake Superior, across my native Upper Peninsula, stopping to see one of the remaining old growth (what we called "virgin timber") areas of forest at Blaney Park, and on into Ontario. My response to the trip was surely affected by boyhood memories, by the observations of relative poverty of many residents, and by the thrill of seeing for the first time the Soo Locks through which the ore boats I had been fascinated to watch in Marquette, Ashland, and Duluth passed from Lake Superior to Lake Huron. We stayed overnight in a motel right on the shore of Whitefish Bay, which had once been traversed by canoes, and could hardly sleep because of the noise of pounding waves during a storm. We went on through Sudbury, where mining activities had made the area look like what we thought the surface of the moon must look like, and then down the beautiful Ottawa River still lined with forest. That part of the trip was experienced through memories of what I had read about the seventeenth-century Jesuits who followed the Hurons and other Native Americans as they engaged in trade and warfare.

Only retrospectively could I sort out the stances of others, past and present, and even the shifts in my own position as we encountered the variety of nature and culture, or cultural penetrations of nature, that we observed. But perhaps underlying the shifts of stance evoked by different facets to which I responded was a position that could be generalized. Since my more idyllic boyhood in the woods and along the lakes and rivers, and even since that trip from west to east across that northern rim of the United States into Ontario, what had always been a disturbance for many persons about the state of the natural environment has now become a global crisis. Naming it a global crisis now affects our perceptions and our stances. The word *crisis* seems to entail a descriptive premise that is at the same time a value premise, whether that creates a philosophical embarrassment of making the naturalistic fallacy or not.

Philosopher Hans Jonas is correct when he wrote that

as long as [a] danger is unknown, we do not know what to preserve and why. Knowledge . . . comes . . . from the perception of what to avoid. *This is perceived first and teaches us, by the revulsion of feeling which acts ahead of knowledge, to apprehend the value whose antithesis so affects us.* We know the thing is at stake only when we know that it is at stake. *Because this is the way we are made: the perception of the* malum *[evil] is infinitely easier to us than the perception of the* bonum *[good].*

Certainly this has been historically true about the emergence of concerns for the environment. Historian Clarence Glacken has demonstrated that concerns for the physical environment as well as ambivalence about those concerns have occurred throughout the history of our culture. He notes, for only one example, that in classical culture there were theories of soil exhaustion interestingly "related to the philosophical idea of the senescence in nature, an application of the organic analogy to the earth itself." Although concern for future generations provoked long and serious discussions by philosophers, theologians, and others only in recent decades, Glacken presents evidences for it long in our past. But throughout, I believe, Jonas's observation is fundamentally correct: humans perceive the threat of an evil outcome before they know what is the good. And, the evil threatened is more clearly justified than the good to be achieved, or even preserved. For this chapter, I also consider Jonas to be correct in saying that there is a revulsion of feeling which acts ahead of knowledge. Thus I will look at revulsions of feelings that motivate concerns for the environment as clues to

24

what we value about it. In the course of this I will try to isolate some antitheses to the perceived evils as a way of saying positively what is valued and why.

Roderick Nash has written a history of *Wilderness and the American Mind* in which he distinguished two distinct sorts of concerns, and these will help structure my argument. One is basically a utilitarian concern: we perceive the deleterious outcomes of various interventions into nature that threaten not only human well-being, but the conditions necessary for sustaining life itself. The other is basically a concern for nature virtually as an end in itself: we perceive threats to what is here in nature because we believe that there is some intrinsic value or good in it. Furthermore, Nash correctly points to mixed feelings and mixed arguments and policies—thus locating where I believe many of us are in our own concerns and responses.

Many years ago I went to Denver to give a speech in the late spring. My hosts put me up in a generic motel on the east side of South Colorado Boulevard. I was attracted to this trip in part because I wanted to see the grandeur of the Rockies, the sight of which I had been deprived for some years. As is my custom, I awakened early and went out to watch the sun rising on the mountains to the west. What did I see? In the foreground were other generic motels and fast-food establishments on the west side of the boulevard, as far as my vision could reach both north and south, and already a considerable amount of automobile traffic. In the background was only a very dim outline of the majestic mountains, for it was one of those days when the combination of weather and urban air pollution created an almost impenetrable haze that even gave slight pain to my eyes as I struggled to view the object of my visual search. I had one of Jonas's revulsion of feelings.

What were these feelings? In this case they were primarily aesthetic feelings. The beauty I anticipated in the distance was opaque; it did not have even the pleasing wisps of fog variously layered against the mountains that one sees so often in Japanese landscape paintings or when one drives across the Appalachians in Tennessee. I could only imagine what I could not see, or I could purchase a picture postcard at the motel desk probably taken from an airplane on a spectacularly clear day and reassure myself that the Rockies really are grand.

The contrast, for me, was the memory of a June evening in Geneva years before when I sat on a bench on the north shore of the western end of Lake Geneva and watched in rapt attention as the sun set on Mont Blanc, with colors changing slowly over a long time. The beauty I anticipated in Denver was obtruded by both natural weather conditions and the effects of modern urban technology; the beauty I experienced in Geneva that day was facilitated by both natural weather conditions and the absence of technological effects. On a more recent visit to Geneva I sought to replicate the scene of twenty-five years before, but never saw Mont Blanc. I hopefully believed it was only the weather.

Not only was the beauty I anticipated in Denver opaque, but there was a foreground ugliness that would have affected my perception even if the Rockies had been clearly in view: the standard architecture of small commercial businesses; the neon signs that assure us whether we are in Denver, Atlanta, or Cleveland, the same fast foods are available; the traffic whizzing past me. Perhaps Andy Warhol and others could make something beautiful out of the commonplaces of commercial technology, but I could not.

So, we have one principal perception of the "evil" to be avoided, one that makes us appreciate a "good" to be enjoyed, namely the presence of ugliness. My Thai Buddhist text applies here; everything exists interdependently—trees, mountains, weather, pollution, even human artifacts within our visual perspective. But what is the proper equilibrium that is the proper condition of all we see? And, it is our affectivity, our feelings, that are first touched. I did not have an aesthetic theory to justify my feelings of beauty that evening in Geneva, or my feelings of revulsion that morning in Denver. Nor could I have analyzed, for lack of knowledge, just what chemical interactions were occurring to obstruct my view from the east side of Colorado Boulevard.

Sometimes, for some persons, "natural" beauty is a combination of what humans and nature make. Some Atlantans wax poetic about its skyline, but that has always passed by me. But Chicago's—that for me is another matter. Driving each Sunday morning for about twelve miles up and back on Lake Shore Drive to church offered weekly a different combination of nature and culture, almost every one of which evoked a sense of the sublime, if not of beauty. A good friend who could spend hours observing the details of the pews in a church in Florence once said, "Lake Michigan is malevolent." But seeing that skyline sometimes in contrast to placid blue waters, sometimes in contrast to violent storms crashing near to the road, that was beauty. We could not resist going to "The Point" at the end of Fifty-fifth Street on a February Sunday when the waves closed Lake Shore Drive and crashed high over the breakers on to the land—the view was awesomely sublime. I had no theory of the equilibrium of all things or the place of the lake and the skyline in it, but I had feelings—the sublime was sometimes awesome, evoking a sense of the powers of that lake not yet fully tamed by humans, and sometimes calming, with the same skyline bathed in the rising sun adding some dimensions to the experience.

The point is that we are concerned about the environment in part because some, or much, of what human activity does to it mars its beauty. Ugliness is repulsive to us; in turn, we value the threatened beauty of the natural world. However, the beauty in nature is often cultured beauty, that which exists because humans have planned how to use nature. A long morning in a Japanese garden in Kyoto gives one a sense of the equilibrium my Buddhist text extols, but if one looks with care and has an experienced guide, one sees trees being trimmed as if they were hair cared for by a stylist in an expensive salon, and one learns how to look at the garden from different angles to see a different equilibrium from different points along the trail. So beauty is not always simply natural; "nature" is sometimes made beautiful by human artistry. Indeed, if I did not continuously trim and cut out nature's growth in the yard upon which I look from my typewriter as I write this, ugliness and destruction would mar and even perhaps destroy a view that nourishes my soul each day. One of the enemy aggressors is kudzu.

Can most of us give a rational justification for preserving or conserving natural environments because we value their beauty? Do we have aesthetic theories, or theories of human nature that would be bulwarks against those who value nature only for its utility to human consumption or economic development? Some of us may, but I am sure most do not. I don't think we would get far by again quoting Genesis—God created all this natural diversity and saw that it was good, indeed very good. "Good" there, even, has an overtone of utility, and nothing is said about beauty.

We are left with a sense of wonder, a sense of the sublime, and maybe even with a sense of the divine. We can quote again the words of my anthropologist colleague Melvin Konner, who after synthesizing much science to explain the nature of the human, waxes poetic, not only about the human ("We must try once again to experience the human soul as soul, and not just as a buzz of bioelectricity, the human will as will, and not just a surge of hormones," etc.) but also the natural world, using as his icon the famous photograph of earth from outer space—"Will we remember what it meant to us? How fine the earth looked, dangled in space? How pretty against the endless black? How round? How very breakable? How small?" No reduction to utility value in these words! Instead he expresses a

30

feeling, a sense of wonder, a sense of the sublime—maybe even (contrary to his atheism) a sense of the divine.

Beauty, it has been argued, is an intrinsic value. It is an end in itself and not a means to any other end. It is not instrumental. I remind you of this argument, but will not pursue it very far. I have never been persuaded by it, since beauty is a value for human beings because we have the capacity to appreciate it. It is a value in relation to human desires and ends, but not likely to the desires and ends of squirrels and red-headed woodpeckers. And to agree on what objects are beautiful to see or hear is not easy; there is no cultural consensus about either what is beautiful in nature or in human products. I can agree with my wife that the cornfields of Iowa in July are beautiful, but more beautiful to me is a lake nestled in the woods and hills on Michigan's Upper Peninsula or inland Maine.

Wilderness, the theme of Nash's study, however, is that which must be tamed, as he clearly states, for the sake of meeting more immediate economic and other human needs. But the threat to the beauty of the natural world causes feelings of revulsion for many; to justify why we value nature, whether in harmonious patterns or "red in tooth and claw" as Tennyson had to say to qualify his romanticism, we might choose to affirm its beauty as an intrinsic value. This is short of the implications of the Genesis creation myth: the diversity of nature is good because God created it to be good, and saw that it is, indeed, very good—what some persons claim is a biblical theological backing for its intrinsic value.

Such theological props are not persuasive to many people in this secular age. So, in addition to arguing beauty as an intrinsic value, we have a large body of literature seeking to answer the question, "Does nature have rights?" Why are we concerned? Because the rights of nature are violated by its wanton exploitation and use by human beings. Again, we have a much-discussed position I will not pursue—but we have an option to be noted. To use rights language is, I think, to propose one of the strongest supports against any kind of external intervention—depending, of course, on how we answer the questions of "whose rights?" and "rights to what?" It is the transfer, in more than metaphoric terms, of a claim in the order of human activity and social life to the nonhuman aspects of nature.

Mary Midgley, in *Animals and Why They Matter*, says that *rights* is a desperate word. I agree with her conclusion, the argument for which cannot be summarized here.

It can be used in a wide sense to draw attention to

*problems, but not to solve them. In its moral sense,
it oscillates uncontrollably between applications
which are too wide to resolve conflicts ("the right to
life, liberty and the pursuit of happiness") and ones
which are too narrow to be plausible ("the basic human right to stay at home on Bank Holiday").*

Again, I suspect, we have feelings of revulsion about
the suffering of animals, the extinction of a beautiful
species, or what have you, just as we are revolted by the
unavailability of medical care to many who need it.
And, our response to the perceived evil is to defend its
counterpart good by claiming that the good has a right
to be realized or preserved.

The rights move to sustain something intrinsically
valued in nature relies upon rational justifications that
might find a sense of the beautiful, or the sublime, to
be intellectually woolly. Rights and duties are most at
home in the sphere of the law, and the law is a place for
logical, very rational discourse. But, at least in some
writers who use rights, or intrinsic value, language
about the natural environment, one finds even explicit
references to religious outlooks. Bill McKibben's widely
read *The End of Nature,* an apocalyptic title since it
refers more to end as *finis* than *telos,* is an example.

Another way of melding an intrinsic element into

justification for our concern comes from the Gaia vision. As commentators indicate, this perception of the interdependence of things on earth as one organism has taken two directions since its introduction. The view is, after all, named for Gaia, the goddess of earth, or in essence, the earth as god. And thus it can be turned to new age mysticism or to more traditional religious usages to stress the presence of the Deity within the creation. Rosemary Radford Ruether's recent *Gaia and God* is a creative contribution to the latter. But it also is turned to serious scientific hypotheses by important biologists, generating imaginative research. I only make what might, or might not, be a superficial observation here, namely that when James Lovelock wanted to take *A New Look at the Earth,* the subtitle to the first book called *Gaia,* it took the name of a goddess to evoke a vision of the health of the whole. Naming anything a god, or for a god, suggests affective overtones and undertones, a sense of the sublime, if not of the divine. Earth as the fecund mother on whom all living things depend is not, in any culture, simply a scientific or rational moral justification of our respect.

Albert Schweitzer, one of the polymath geniuses of earlier decades of this century, made popular the notion of reverence for life. Now, the word *reverence* is hard to use without religious, or at least deeply affective, tones. Schweitzer was accused by more orthodox Christian theologians of being a nature mystic, of ignoring the historic distinction between the creator and sustainer of all things and that which was created. For Schweitzer, the reverence for life was based more on borrowings from Arthur Schopenhauer than orthodox theology, on the belief that everything has a will to live. Of course, orthodox Roman Catholic thomistic theology affirmed that; it is a natural end and object in all things. But orthodox theology set the will to live of all things in a hierarchy in which the lower life forms existed to serve the needs of the higher; we, being the highest form of created things except for angels, could use the lower for our own proper ends. It was this hierarchy that Schweitzer, in principle, denied. Thus the practical outcome came close to Jainism, and clearly Schweitzer's studies of the religions of Asia influenced him. Perhaps like rights, reverence raises a useful question, but the answer does not resolve forced choices in policies or personal life. However, it does posit something intrinsic—not beauty, but will. Why be concerned? Because not to be is to tread upon the intrinsic will of all natural things to live.

Other discussions of additional justifications for

viewing the natural world as being intrinsically, and not simply instrumentally, valuable, are not considered here.

I turn to Nash's other stream, namely answers to the question of why we are concerned that are finally instrumental, or finally in relation to utility value for humans, or in some cases for the wider spheres of nature of which we are a part.

Why are we concerned? Because of threats to the quality of life we enjoy in our place and our time. I stress here the words *quality of life* and the possessive adjective *our* to indicate the problematics of this view. First, what qualities of life are threatened? One could, I suppose, conduct a poll to substantiate quantitatively just what qualities of life any particular group of people values. One can guess, at least, that the qualities are those that meet our immediate gratification of various desires. And in urbanized, industrial societies—not simply any longer only those of the so-called West—it takes technology and availability of items for consumption way beyond the needs of survival to gratify us. If one visits Stockholm or Bangkok, Toronto or Kuala Lumpur, for all their differences one is overwhelmed by similarities—heavy automobile traffic, air-conditioned high-rise buildings, generic fast-food places, and hotels managed so that an American can "feel at home" in

Kuala Lumpur. (On a trip to Malaysia for the government recently I received a booklet about how to get around in its capital city. One paragraph explained that the safest way to cross a busy street is to get in the middle of a group of Malaysians and stay with their flow.)

The limit point can be reasonably projected. If we are concerned about environment to maintain the quality of consumption we all enjoy, the dependence on nature of that quality might deplete, if not exhaust, the necessary conditions for our enjoyment. While I read arguments that scientific and technological ingenuity and market forces will be sufficient to resolve any projected doomsdays, even considering population growth, I have not been assured that nature can sustain *our* quality of life for the more than five billion people now inhabiting the earth. So, in principle, we are faced with the need for restraints that probably entail limits on availability of what meets our desires, even for the sake of meeting them.

Who is included in the "our" quality of life? Some of us might remember discussions of about three decades ago concerning whether, for example, Americans had any obligations to less developed parts of the earth. The crassest (no doubt a judgment involved in using that word) proposal was that we did not, and that if the survival of our quality of life was detrimental to others, so be it. (When I was in the army, we had more vivid words for "so be it" and it was not "Amen," but it might be indiscreet to use them here.) And we know that if the "our" includes even all the residents of our nation, there are too many among us far more deprived than the middle classes of nations less wealthy than our own. This is why the issue of justice is raised in discussions of environmental ethics. The "our" is sociocentric—not even biocentric—and fairness of distribution of both benefits and restraints or suffering is a matter to be taken seriously.

Why are we concerned? Because, in apocalyptic versions, the survival of our species might be endangered. Surely the perceived evil of the greenhouse effect is in part the harm it can cause to human life, in simply a biological sense, as well as to other forms of life. This sort of response is sometimes called species-centric. It has some scientific grounding in the descriptive and explanatory accounts given us by naturalists, by biologists who focus on more than genes, enzymes, and other microscopic aspects of nature. It can even be supported by some classic religious-philosophic positions: every entity, including the human species, is oriented toward its well-being, and survival is a necessary condition for that well-being. It is a strongly future-oriented concern; while, as Glacken shows, concern for the well-being of future generations is not utterly novel historically, certainly a threat to it has sharpened our concern for the environment. Evidence for this can be found by even a limited literature search. There were few articles about obligations to future generations by philosophers and theologians until about thirty years ago; since then the justification for such concerns has occupied the attention of many scholars from various disciplines. If one wishes to judge the moral quality of various instrumental justifications for our concern, this one is surely more inclusive and generous, maybe even more just, than justifying our concern only on the effects that threats would have to our consumer culture's quality of life.

Why be concerned? Another instrumental view is that the preservation of biodiversity is important, maybe even essential, for the continuation of many forms of life which may or may not be of utilitarian value to us—now or ever. E. O. Wilson has made this case in a detailed and masterful way. This position is often called biocentrism. The center of value is not quality of life, not merely our species, but all of life, *including* our species. More immediate justifications can be given. Resources for the development of medications can be found in plants that are threatened; potential new food sources exist and would be necessary if our domesticated grains were somehow threatened. The development of seed banks in various parts of the world is a response to this.

Biocentrism is far more inclusive, but not unrelated to species-centrism. Gaia as an icon for biocentrism, or the earth as "God's body" as discussed by Sallie McFague, becomes attractive even though it invites heresy in traditional theology because of the emphasis on the immanence and not transcendence of the Deity. Reverence for life, Wilson's "biophilia," or at least respect for all that lives, takes on a deeper justification and plausibility.

I have briefly suggested three forms of more instrumental or utilitarian responses to the question, "Why are we concerned?" Each of these as a stance toward the environment would become, with further development, the basis for different lines of moral direction for our consumer habits, for what limits might be put on human interventions into nature, and for environmental policy and law. Each is a moral stance toward nature, just as the aesthetic, the rights language, and others are, which are based on the more intrinsic value side of a continuum of moral stances. Do these various rational answers to the question fully exhaust why we are concerned? Or is there, in many of us at least, a sense of the sublime, or even a sense of the divine in nature—noted as mingled in some stances I have mentioned?

The answer to that question is empirical, and I do not have decisive evidence to indicate how widespread the sense of the sublime or the divine is among persons interested in environmental ethics. One cannot read Aldo Leopold, John Muir, and others without some awareness that it exists. Historically, it carries more than echoes of nineteenth-century romanticism, of Emerson and the New England transcendentalists, or of Rousseau and Goethe. But in Jessica Mathews's book *Preserving the Global Environment*, there is not even a trace of it; the issues are all developed in the language of law, policy, and economics. (I shall return to this book subsequently.) Konner's sense of wonder is stipulated very self-consciously in nonreligious terms, but surely his sense of the sublime shows through. Hans Jonas appeals to the sense of revulsion which evokes concern and provides a metaphysical account for the concern, but avoids using language that might be judged to be theological or religious.

To be sure, there are various theological interpretations, many coming from the process theology group, for example, Jay McDaniel's *Of God and Pelicans* and John Cobb's many contributions, with others coming from more biblically grounded positions. Richard R. Niebuhr, among others, reminds readers of John Calvin's natural sense of divinity in his idea of nature as the theater of God's glory. Readers of Jonathan Edwards are often moved by his perception of aspects of nature as images and shadows of divine things. And, while the argument for the existence of God from the design of nature, the so-called Book of Nature that can be read alongside the book of special revelation, has been hard put since Kant and the onslaught of evolutionary theories, with careful circumscription it continues to appear, for example, in Stephen Toulmin, *The Return to Cosmology*. Often it is more as explication of an experience of the divine than evidence for a rational argument to prove that God exists.

I adduce here reactions like Konner's and similar ones. In 1992 the seminar I conducted for Emory faculty members was on "Nature." The twelve participants each came from a different discipline or professional school in the university. We read literature—Wordsworth and Tennyson, Goethe and Longus—and philosophers—Jonas, Toulmin, John Dewey, and Erazim Kohák. We read creation accounts from the ancient near east, including biblical ones. We read accounts of biological, physical, and social scientific theories. And we read the Mathews book, mentioned above, and other works on policy. Not all responses were the same to anything we read, as one might expect. Wordsworth's *Prelude* was too romantic; Tennyson's *In Memoriam* showed a man caught between a romantic religious view and the effects of reading Lyell's historical geology; Mathews was too couched in policy jargon, and so on. At the end we talked about which of the books were most impressive and why. Interestingly, Kohák's *The Embers and the Stars,* a philosophic, poetic, and religious reflection on nature, came to the fore. Some thought Kohák was really Thoreau revisited in spite of his efforts to distinguish his position from Thoreau's; some were offended by the introduction of God language; some felt he did not interpret what science he used correctly and wished he had better scientific backing for the work. But what was impressive in the end was that no one thought these reflections to be totally silly; all, I believe, were strangely moved by Kohák's evocation of a moral sense of nature, and even sense of divinity through our participation in nature. A biophysicist and a primatologist both said, "I like that, but I wish I could prove it."

Like my Thai monk, for Kohák everything exists interdependently. All the participants in my seminar, including me, thought Kohák had underplayed conflict and destructive forces in nature. We were in general agreement that my anti-text from the Thai monk, "Anything which exists in a proper condition is in equilibrium with everything else," was echoed in Kohák's book. In astronomy and biology, in life experience with forces of nature, conflict and destruction mar the harmony that is romantically appealing. If there is a sense of divinity, it has to include not only dependence upon nature for beauty and for sustenance, but also forces beyond human control which destroy each other and us. If God saw that the diversity God created was good, it was not *necessarily* good for humans and for all aspects of nature.

What is finally indisputable, I think, is that human and other forms of life are dependent upon forces we do not create and cannot fully control, forces that bring us into being and sustain us and life around us, but forces that also limit and destroy us and determine the destiny of the cosmos. This dependence—a matter of fact, no matter how it is interpreted—evokes a sense of the sublime, or for some of us a sense of the divine. In the Book of Job we have the best biblical account of the ambiguity of natural powers, relative to a human perception of what is good, and a most honest and honorable ambivalence toward the Divine.

John Calvin wrote, "I confess, of course, that it can be said reverently, provided that it proceeds from a reverent mind, that nature is God. . . ." Quickly he points out that God should not be confused with the inferior course of God's works and proceeds to tell us that this sense of the divine can become a factory of idols, that only in Scripture is there true knowledge of God. We have to be fair to Calvin. But the confession is telling. Through the powers of nature humans have a sense of the divine. That is an affective as well as rational sense. Nature is the theater of the power and glory of the Divine. It provides a moral stance.

My discussion has now reached the theocentric perspective. As I noted in the introduction, it has been amply criticized on various confessional and philosophical theological grounds, as well as epistemological and other more purely philosophical ones. The position has been accused of naiveté in the use of materials from science, an accusation I reject. "Why not say that God is Nature and Nature is God?" I am asked. Is the transcendence of God satisfactorily defended since monotheism is affirmed? Is the view finally fideistic, taking a leap not warranted by the evidences adduced from nature and human experience? Is there a gap in the trail between the common sense ontology of interdependence and the affirmation of an ultimate orderer and power? In some contexts of discussion I have to answer these queries as best I can, though never persuasively to my critics, but my fate in this regard is no worse than the fate of my critics, about whose work similar or other questions can be asked.

Perhaps the best metaphoric description of the technical structure of the position is that of a raft, as suggested by John P. Reeder. Like the Coca-Cola sign fishing raft we used on Brown's Lake in Dickinson County, Michigan, there are four barrels, one in each corner: evidences from relevant sciences (and never "science" as one reified whole), human experience, philosophical judgments, and the heritage of Christianity and Judaism as continued in those traditions. All are necessary, and none is sufficient, but the raft tips to one corner or another depending upon the weight of the exposition and defense. We leave these matters for other contexts.

The theocentric perspective, deeply informed as it is by the Bible and traditions which flow from it, probably evokes, better than it explains. I have no serious quarrels with Mary Midgley, Melvin Konner, and many earlier writers who have similar moral stances toward the nature but are agnostics or declared atheists. Their senses of wonder, appreciation, respect for nature, and their willingness to allow this to suffice is more comfortable to my thinking and living than are the systematic debates in which I also must be engaged. I cannot persuasively argue that their stances entail the acknowledgment of God or gods, nor do I wish even to try. Even as I attempt to come to better resolutions of the intellectual ambiguities of theocentrism as I have delineated it, Wordsworth and Kohák and many others inform my "moral sense of nature" as Kohák subtitles his book.

The contingencies as well as ordering of the natural world, the elements of conflict, and perhaps even chaos, within it, as well as the elements of harmony thrust me, and perhaps others, into a sense of ultimate dependence upon the powers, and (if it be a leap of faith, so be it) the power of God. Functionally, in an intellectual mode as well as in a spiritual one, to live and act in a theocentric perspective is to know and feel the relativities of all other centers of value proposed by my fellow interpreters of the natural environment. It has so put a face on what is ultimately mystery, to note Gordon Kaufman's book again. It is, and this is where the theocentrism I affirm is accused of heterodoxy and even heresy by more orthodox theologians and pastors, to acknowledge that the source and power and order of all of nature is not always beneficent in its outcomes for the diversity of life and for the well-being of humans as part of that. More orthodox theologies than mine do not deny natural as well as moral, social, and other evils, but finally on the basis of Christian revelation proclaim the triumph of the good. I think, however, that in the face of environmental and other crises we all are practically engaged in what Hans Jonas described as a perception of the evil and revulsion against it as the first order of thought and action.

A theocentric perspective informs and empowers a sense of radical dependence and a consciousness of the ambiguities of the many relations of multiple values of things for each other in nature. It does not require a cosmological view of an open and extending universe to make us conscious of the possibilities of human action to restrain various effects which can be judged by us humans to be undesirable, deleterious, or even evil in both the very natural ordering of things and our participation in nature. It makes us conscious of the potentiality for benefits through our justifiable interventions, but at the same time conscious of our limits to control all the outcomes in accord with our praiseworthy intentions. "God is in the details." Hope, the conditions of possibility for preserving and enhancing what we can justifiably value, is in the details, and its realization demands our response to particular details. These themes, I warn, will recur as we move forward in this book.

God is the source of human good but does not guarantee it. My Thai monk is wrong, not in his first affirmation but in his second, namely that "anything that exists in a proper condition is in equilibrium with everything else." The moral stance of the religious view I am affirming pays deeply its respect to nature, but since conflict or dissonance, as well as harmony and consonance are part of nature and our place in it, the moral stance itself does not resolve environmental ethical issues. The purposes of nature, relative to "anything that exists" and to the interdependence of all, are conflictual relative to the human good and even various "goods" of the nonhuman world. We have to ask, "Good for what?" "Good for whom?" and when we do, we are ready for the second chapter.

References and Bibliographical Notes

Hans Jonas, *The Imperative of Responsibility* (Chicago: University of Chicago Press, 1984), is a careful exploration of how we incrementally drift in a technological age to points of no return for aspects of nature; it is a "heuristics of fear" written in a quiet mode. The quotation is from page 27. Clarence J. Glacken, *Traces on the Rhodian Shore* (Berkeley: University of California Press, 1967), provides an encyclopedic account of Western thought about the relations of culture and nature from classical times to the nineteenth century; the quotation is from page 134, and many more citations are

49

possible for the point made here. Roderick Nash, *Wilderness and the American Mind*, 3d ed. (New Haven: Yale University Press, 1982), includes discussions of political and policy issues as well as literature. Tennyson, *In Memoriam A. H. H.*, stanza 56: "Man . . . Who trusted God was love indeed / And love Creation's final law—/ Tho' Nature, red in tooth and claw / With ravine, Shriek'd against his creed—. . . ." The quotation from Mary Midgley can be found in *Animals and Why They Matter* (Harmondsworth: Penguin, 1983), 63. Bill McKibben's *The End of Nature* (New York: Random House, 1989) and other writings established him as one of the most influential nature writers in recent times. If my book were in focus more on differences among theologies of the natural world than it is, Rosemary Radford Ruether's *Gaia and God: An Ecofeminist Theology of Earth Healing* (San Francisco: Harper and Row, 1992) would be an important book to discuss. *Gaia: A New Look at the Earth* by James Lovelock (New York: Oxford University Press, 1987) is one of those generative books that brings new icons or symbols into discussions and thus enriches them. Specific citations of Schweitzer's work are given in chapter 4. E. O. Wilson's most thorough discussion is found in *The Diversity of Life* (Cambridge: Harvard University Press, 1992). Sallie McFague's book *God's Body* is announced but not available at the time of this writing, but see her *Models of God: Theology for an Ecological, Nuclear Age* (Philadelphia: Fortress Press, 1987), 69–78. Wilson's "biophilia" describes a stance toward the natural world with the affective overtones of love for it; see Wilson, *Biophilia* (Cambridge: Harvard University Press, 1984). Aldo Leopold's *A Sand County Almanac* (New York:

Oxford University Press, 1949) remains a classic rich in insights which combine a stance with other dimensions. Roderick Nash's chapter on him is titled "Aldo Leopold: Prophet," in *Wilderness,* 182–99; his chapter on Muir is "John Muir: Publicizer," 123–40. For a beautifully written account (not referred to in the text of this chapter) of how the different "stances," or interests and desires, affect the imaging and use of the arctic region of North America, see Barry Lopez, *Arctic Dreams: Imagination and Desire in a Northern Landscape* (New York: Scribners, 1986); Lopez shows the difference in significance of the same region to the Inuits, the explorers, the exploiters of resources, etc. Jessica Tuchman Mathews, ed., *Preserving the Global Environment: The Challenge of Shared Leadership* (New York: W. W. Norton & Co., 1991), is discussed in Chapter Four. Jay B. McDaniel, *Of God and Pelicans: A Theology of Reverence for Life* (Louisville: Westminster/John Knox Press, 1989), in addition to its well-wrought constructive argument, contains a useful bibliography. McDaniel made notable contributions to the development of ecological concerns in the World Council of Churches. Among Cobb's many contributions are two coauthored books, each done with a specialist in a different area: Charles Birch and John B. Cobb, Jr., *The Liberation of Life: From Cell to Community* (Cambridge: Cambridge University Press, 1981), written with a biologist who, like McDaniel, made great contributions to the World Council of Churches, and Herman E. Daly and John B. Cobb, Jr., *For the Common Good: Redirecting the Economy Toward Community and Environment, and a Sustainable Future* (Boston: Beacon Press, 1989), written with an economist. The latter book is one of the most carefully developed efforts to "close the circle" that I have referred to. Richard R. Niebuhr contributes "the unconventional compound *theo-graphia*" in his article, "The Tent of Heaven," published in *The Alumni Bulletin of Bangor Theological Seminary* 52 (1977–78): 9–22. The article closes with a discussion of Calvin on nature as the theater of God's glory. For a careful analysis of this theme in Calvin, see Susan E. Schreiner, *The Theater of His Glory: Nature and the Natural Order in the Thought of John Calvin* (Durham, N.C.: The Labyrinth Press, 1991). For relevant discussions of Jonathan Edwards, see Sang Hyun Lee, "Mental Activity and the Perception of Beauty in Jonathan Edwards," *Harvard Theological Review* 69 (1976): 369–96, and Roland DeLattre, *Beauty and Sensibility in the Thought of Jonathan Edwards* (New Haven: Yale University Press, 1958). See also Edwards, *Images and Shadows of Divine Things* (Westport, Conn.: Greenwood Press, 1977), and various materials in Jonathan Edwards, *Scientific and Philosophical Writings* (New Haven: Yale University Press, 1980). Stephen Toulmin's turn to theology is found in *The Return to Cosmology: Postmodern Science and the Theology of Nature* (Berkeley: University of California Press, 1982), 217–74. Kohák's book is *The Embers and the Stars: A Philosophical Inquiry into the Moral Sense of Nature* (Chicago: The University of Chicago Press, 1984). For an awesomely haunting account of the destructive power of natural forces, not referred to in the text, see Norman Maclean, *Young Men and Fire* (Chicago: University of Chicago Press, 1992), an account of the death of parachute-jumping forest-fire fighters trapped in a lightning-ignited blaze. Maclean writes, "It is easy for us to assume that as a result of modern science 'we have conquered nature,' . . . But we should be prepared for the possibility . . . that the terror of the universe has not yet fossilized and the universe has not run out of blowups" (46). For this favorite sentence of mine from John Calvin, see *The Institutes of the Christian Religion*, I, 5, 5, John T. McNeill, ed., 2 vols. (Philadelphia: Westminster Press, 1955), 1:58. Reeder's discussion of the raftlike structure of my work is found in Beckley and Swezey (119–37), cited here in my introduction. For Mary Midgley's account of humanism, see, "The Paradox of Humanism," in Beckley and Swezey, 187–99.

2

Human Accountability
The Inevitability of Moral Ambiguity

In the first chapter I described various moral stances toward nature, particularly emphasizing bipolar extremes. One extreme is that nature has intrinsic value or rights, that nature itself is sacred, that our attitude toward it ought to be reverence. The other extreme was utilitarian, that nature is there for our use and benefits as human beings. The point on which I closed, namely that from a theocentric perspective nature evokes in us a sense of the sublime, or more religiously, a sense of the divine, calls for *respect* for nature. I stressed the conflictual as well as harmonious aspects of nature itself, which left us with questions of "Good for whom?" and "Good for what?"

While any moral stance is not sufficient to answer those questions when we are confronted by particular choices, one's stance does make a difference. I want briefly to illustrate this with an experience I had with graduate students in biology at Emory University.

I spent two hours with about thirty students discussing the word *nature*, its various references in Western thought and culture, and the ways in which it can and cannot become a basis for certain moral judgments. The students quickly focused on part of the subtitle of Kohák's book *The Embers and the Stars*: "the moral sense of nature." Given their budding careers, the principal location of the discussion was the use of animals in experimentation.

Three positions were strongly argued. One was by a man on the "intrinsic" side of the polarity. Affectively, emotionally, he was drawn to a kind of Albert Schweitzer view of nature, maybe even a Jainist view. All animals (we did not talk about plants) have a will to live and thus to harm them and take their lives raises serious moral questions. His intuition was that all animal life, at least, is of equal value. If he could be persuaded that there was a justifiable hierarchy of values in nature he could pursue his doctoral studies in biology with a better conscience.

The second man took a rather purely utilitarian view, claiming for its support what he called the classical and Judeo-Christian position of Western culture.

56

The lower exists for the sake of the higher: plants exist for the sake of animals and humans, and animals exist for the sake of humans. Thus, experimentation on animals, including disposing of them, is justified if there are any long- or short-range benefits for human beings. Benefits, whatever they might be, justify the means used to realize them.

The third position was taken by a Hindu neurobiologist, newly arrived from Bombay. On the basis of religious tradition and conviction she is a vegetarian but experiments with rats, which she has to "sacrifice" (not merely "dispose of") in the course of her work. She recognized the apparent inconsistency of her position in comparison with her two colleagues, and in effect said that the bifurcation of her responses to nature was a practical necessity for her scientific objectives.

These young scientists already know from their experience what Stephen Toulmin, among others, has observed.

> [T]he pure scientist's traditional posture as theoros, or spectator, can no longer be maintained: we are always—and inescapably—participants or agents as well. . . . Instead of viewing the world of nature as onlookers from outside, we now have to understand how our own human life and activities operate as elements within the world of nature. So we must de-

velop a more coordinated view of the world, embracing both the world of nature and the world of humanity. . . .

Participants is the key word I want to stress here. Theologian Richard R. Niebuhr makes the same point about knowledge: "Construed as creative action, knowing is participatory rather than mimetic or representational action. It draws from the sources of life and 'pays back' to the common life the 'dividend' of an augmented, enlarged, more generous self." Humans are interactive participants in the ordering of the natural world. This is amply clear in ordinary life; only recently have philosophers and others argued that it is also the case in scientific investigations of nature. But the epistemology of the sciences is not our interest in these chapters.

I must look at some trivialities to describe a case I want to make, namely that aspects of the nonhuman natural world, as well as humans, interactively participate in other aspects of that world, and a way to interpret that participation which introduces the value term *good* is to ask what and whose goods are served, and at what cost or benefit to what other goods.

I only need to raise my eyes from my typewriter to my backyard to make some trivial points. The English ivy is progressing down the hill at a rate of about four to

58

eight feet a year, choking out the fescue that the contractors planted to restrain erosion caused by the grading required to build our home. The dominance of the English ivy is desirable for us; it is lovely to look at and requires minimal care, though I spent hours tracing honeysuckle vines to their taproots and digging them out. While the fescue does not have the capacity to complain, surely it is naturally oriented toward continuing in life and would do so without the participation of the ivy in this ecological niche.

When I walk to Emory University I daily see how kudzu has grown up to and flourishes at the tops of some pines and tulip poplars that are over one hundred feet high. I know those trees will die if someone does not cut out and kill the kudzu, kill it with the gardener's favorite herbicide, "Roundup." But some of the natural forms that kudzu takes even as it kills those trees are beautiful enough to compete with the carefully sculpted Japanese gardens one finds in Golden Gate Park in San Francisco or in Kyoto. What is not good for the trees is good for the kudzu, and what is good for the kudzu can evoke ambivalence in the human observer; the vine is an aggressor (we cannot say "unjust" because it is not capable of intentional action) that destroys trees (which we favor), but it also produces silhouettes as aesthetically admirable as some produced by land-

59

scape artists. Humans have to make a choice about which is the aggressor and which is the victim, and the choice involves answering the questions, "Good for whom?" and "Good for what?" One might like to believe the author of the first chapter of Genesis and say that kudzu, pine and tulip trees, English ivy and fescue are good because they exist. But such a belief ignores the costly and beneficial participation of aspects of nature in other aspects of nature.

Hans Jonas points out in *The Phenomenon of Life,* a philosophical interpretation of biology, how the emergence of creatures with the capacity to move about added a different sequence to the story of development. Plants, to be sure, migrate, but animals migrate faster, and their mobility enables them to invade and use not only plants but other animals to meet their needs for survival. The food chain is one phenomenon we all know about that makes this clear.

If I raise myself forward and turn to the left I can see on our deck some feathers of a mourning dove that was attracted to our bird feeder, but killed by one of the cats that is attracted to the birds. The kind of feeder we have is in part accountable for the occasional killing of a dove. I set the balance on it so that the feeder closes from the weight of squirrels and doves and sometimes blue jays, but never does from small birds. This consigns the doves, who seem not to be as alert as other birds anyway, to being scavengers on the floor and thus subject to cunning feline predation. If I see a cat lurking on the top step to the deck I scare it off, but I cannot be a scare-cat all the time. The cat and the dove are all doing what comes naturally, participating in nature, augmented by human action and devices. My preference of whose good should be realized there are clear—birds above cats. They differ from the cat's preferences. Why do I prefer the "good" of a dove to the what is "good" for the cat?

Perhaps some readers have seen the Swedish film *My Life as a Dog*. If you have, you might remember the central character, a boy growing up in all sorts of unpleasant or ambiguous circumstances and events, most of which lead to misery for his life. So he keeps thinking about the dog that the Soviets sent up in a sputnik, no doubt dead, but revolving around and around the earth, and keeps saying, "Man måste jämfora," "One has to compare." What was beneficial for the development of science was certainly not beneficial for the dog (but the Soviets did not send up a human at that stage), and the boy's own miseries seem survivable, if not tolerable, in comparison to those of the dog.

When we observe the participation of some aspects of nonhuman life in those of other aspects, we must compare. And when we try to think through human accountability in our participation in nature we necessarily compare, whether we are like the first biology graduate student who was attracted to an equal value for at least all living animals, or the second who took a straightforward utilitarian view. Even the third, the Hindu vegetarian neurobiologist, compared, and she at least "sacrifices" her rats rather than "disposes" of them. But she probably "disposes" of the food plant remnants left in the cage when the experiment is over.

Each of the moral stances sets, or frames, the parameters within which comparisons of value choices are made by each of the students. But the particular choices are not determined by the stances. Would the first student be in biology if he did not think something would benefit from research, if only his intellectual curiosity and pleasure? Would the second student agree to animal experimentation which was done simply for the sake of doing whatever one could do to animals, with no other benefits for knowledge? Would the Hindu neurobiologist be ready to live with her contradictory outlooks if she did not think that it was important to know more about how brains, as organs, function? The stances do not resolve the quandaries that arise on the margins of acceptability. One has to compare, make judgments, and give reasons for them. The judgments are made, in my interpretation, about how one answers "Good for whom?" and "Good for what?" and these answers are value-laden. We humans, unlike English ivy and kudzu and cats, are intentional participants. We are purposive unlike kudzu but like cats (kudzu does not stalk pine trees like cats stalk doves); we are intentional in a way cats are not.

All these trivial illustrations are meant to put flesh on some abstract ideas about how the various things valued, by humans consciously or implicitly, and by nonhumans without the same conscious intention, are always in relation to each other. I make the same point differently; from these trivial observations we can develop a more general perspective about the nature of valuing and values.

The theologian H. Richard Niebuhr, who was influenced by, among other things, the American pragmatic philosophers, calls this "relational" value theory. I quote a summary sentence: "Thus relational value theory is concerned with the great multi-dimensionality of value, which is not the multidimensionality of an abstract realm of essential values but rather the multidimensionality of beings in their relations to each other." The world is one of the things in interactive, interdependent relations to each other (my Thai Buddhist text, remember). These relations are value rela-

63

tions, and in at least a loose sense always moral relations. Whatever one might argue about the intrinsic value of the "essence" of something (whatever the "essence" refers to), all beings are sources of *values,* or potential values (I would make plural what Niebuhr makes singular in the quotation), to other beings. Beings—kudzu, cats, humans—have potentialities for various relations that are of value or "disvalue" to other beings; indeed, their specific value or "disvalue" emerges in their specific relations to other things. This richness is what Niebuhr means by the multidimensionality of value.

In a more specifically theological treatise the same author wrote,

Nor can the will of God be interpreted so that it applies within a world of rational beings and not in the world of the unrational, so that men must be treated as ends because they are reasonable but nonhuman life may be violated in their service of human ends. Sparrows and sheep and lilies belong within the network of moral relations when God reveals himself; now every killing is a sacrifice.

The animals used by the graduate students in biology may have value (if some anthropomorphism is permitted) in relation to themselves in that there is a "will" to live in them. But in other interactive relations they have other values; they are sources of knowledge extracted by human interventions into their lives by being placed in controlled environments and subjected to various human actions. That knowledge is costly to the animals, but, one hopes, has value not only by increasing the bulk of what is known but also for humans and perhaps other living things. With regard to the English ivy I see through my window—it has aesthetic value to humans, it has labor-saving value to me, it has to be pruned back from pine trees and azalea bushes because it threatens their lives and thus threatens *their* value of beauty to me, it kills out the fescue which would thrive without its being present.

"Now every killing is a sacrifice," H. Richard Niebuhr wrote. The Hindu student is correct to continue language that was commonplace for many years in scientific studies. Often we used to read, "The animal was sacrificed" in order to gain knowledge. Potentiality for some values is sacrificed for valuations that seem to trump the continued existence of the animal. Moral ambiguity and even an element of the tragic are almost always present when we have good reasons to take life; the outcomes are costly to beings that have value for other beings and are worthy of respect because they exist. The tragic sense probably does not occur to us when we use pesticide to get rid of a wasp's nest where our grandchildren play in our yard or kill a tick we find attached to our bare arm, but it does become more real when we intentionally deprive some other beings, including humans, of relations which would be of value to them for the sake of something we think is of greater value. For example, we justify homicide in war for the sake of peace, justice, liberty.

I have often thought of life in a family as analogous to what goes on in the natural world, with aspects interacting and participating in other aspects. The well-being of an individual member, whether in traditional or newer forms of family life, does not necessarily serve the well-being of other members, or the family unit as a whole—its common good. The good of the parts are not always in equilibrium with each other, and the common good of the whole is not always in harmony with the legitimate ends and aspirations if its parts—individual members of the family. Choices are made which sometimes benefit others and sometimes benefit the common good, but other choices are made which are costly to others. There is moral ambiguity. And it is often necessary to restrain one's own aspirations for legitimate ends for the sake of another's, or for the sake of the well-being of the whole family. Restraint, if this is not too dramatically said, is often a sacrifice of one's own interests for the sake of another's, or of another's for the sake of one's own. By living together we necessarily participate in each others lives; sometimes we actively intervene and other times we consciously forbear. Our capacities to intervene or to forbear are the grounds of our accountability; our affections and desires as well as our reasons for particular actions are subject to some moral evaluation. If there is equilibrium, its form is dynamic, ever changing, and never perfect.

As in the family, so in nature there is interdependence without equilibrium. Recall my Buddhist anti-text: "Anything which exists in a proper condition is in equilibrium with everything else." This is *dhamma*. It tends to assume a condition of stasis, perhaps even of a metaphysical order of perpetual harmony. Bhikkhu Buddhadāsa was concerned, of course, with the disruptions of that harmony that are caused by increasingly radical interventions, indeed interruptions, in that harmonious order—for example, the deforestation going on in Thailand. (The American-Thai symposium on the environment in which I participated had to be moved from one venue to another on rather short notice. Ironically, the first site was badly destroyed by a landslide caused by recent clear-cutting of the mountains in which it was set.) If there is equilibrium, even

67

as an ideal in nature, it is a dynamic one. Such equilibrium as develops changes as different species enter and adapt to new ecological niches. If there is equilibrium in the family, it is also dynamic, changing with changing ages, with external conditions, with activities of its members, and so forth. If there is a dynamic equilibrium (even, and at all) in civil societies the forces that enhance it or disrupt it are many and varied. Surely some believe that the free market is the invisible hand that will work; others who are concerned about distributive or social justice have a very different principle in mind to promote the good of persons and the common good.

Humans, informed increasingly with knowledge of natural processes and constructing technologies and procedures to intervene in nature for various ends, we all know, have degrees of accountability for the outcomes in nature that are unprecedented. If we could say that there is one supreme human good which even ideally would be in harmony with one good of the natural world, then our thinking, if not our acting, would be easier. The multidimensionality of value, or values, that I spoke of, casts us into ambiguities of choices that are unavoidable. We may be able to define limits beyond which our interventions ought not to go, though agreement on these is difficult because different persons or groups value different things in relation to themselves or to the natural world. The following illustration will clarify this point.

Sociologists Renée Fox and Judith Swazey have been tracing the developments in transplantation of organs into humans ever since the technology was developed and have been assessing the ethical, economic, social, and physical outcomes of these procedures. Very recently they published an article, "Leaving the Field," provoked in part by the recent efforts in Pittsburgh to transplant the liver of a baboon into a human patient. The editor appropriately highlights two sentences from the article. "The field of organ replacement now epitomizes a very different and powerful tendency in the American health care system and in the value and belief system of our society's culture: our pervasive reluctance to accept limits to the biological and human condition imposed by the aging process and our ultimate mortality." In other words, technology seeks to overcome biological processes, and in their view some of its medical users are unwilling to consent to the inevitability of aging and death. The implication is that nature—aging and death—ought to be recognized as biological conditions that will have their way, and that medical technology should at some point acquiesce to these realities, thus limiting itself. The other sentence sets the pursuit of the value of longevity and the resources required to realize it in relation to other needs. "One of the most urgent value questions is whether, as poverty, homelessness, and lack of access to health care increase in our affluent country, it is justifiable for American society to be devoting so much of its intellectual energy and human and financial resources to the replacement of human organs." Fox and Swazey have made choices; they have set some things that are valued in relation to the real limits of nature in the first sentence, and in relation to what they judge to be more essential needs of humans in the second. The second is evoked by revulsion in the face of perceived injustice; it is unfair that fundamental needs of many persons are not met while vast resources are used to meet the needs of a few.

Illustrations like this could be spelled out in vast numbers: the spotted owl versus the jobs of timber workers, etc. When some human intervention appears to approach the point of no return for something that is valued supremely or almost supremely, the choice is posed as either/or. When technology as a whole is seen to have enduring deleterious effects in nature, it can become the "demon" and the literature can become apocalyptic. Hans Jonas deliberately uses what he calls "the heuristics of fear," that is, he spells out worst-case scenarios in order to provoke a sense of responsibility of the natural world. Leon Kass, in a discussion not of the natural world as a whole, but of the medical technology of in-vitro fertilization—a microcosm of the issue— writes that, "Our society is dangerously close to losing its grip on the meaning of some fundamental aspects of human existence." The point of citing Kass is this: for him not only is "nature," the human body as an aspect of nature, affected by the increasingly deep technological interventions; more important is that some things he values about the meaning of human life are thus put in peril. That assumes, does it not, that some vision of the value and meaning of human life has to be set in relation to our interventions into nature, and in so doing a restraint would be put on those interventions? That living within certain natural constraints sustains valued qualities of human life?

One could cite more apocalyptic interpretations than those given by Jonas and Kass; for example, Bill McKibben, in his popular *The End of Nature,* seeks to interpret as much of the technical knowledge of the environmental crisis as he can in such a way that our choices are radicalized. And, as a good writer he has had success in increasing awareness of the radical choices. Indeed, in the American-Thai symposium the devout Buddhists loved his presentation. The developmental economists were not as enthusiastic.

My theocentric perspective, humans and other aspects of nature as participants, the multidimensionality of values and relational value theory, and the unavoidability of moral ambiguity all cohere. God is the ultimate power and orderer of the interdependence of elements of life with each other. But there is no clear overriding telos, or end, which unambiguously orders the priorities of nature and human participation in it so that one has a perfect moral justification for all human interventions. I said "all" because, in some cases, such as the apparent eradication of the small pox virus from human populations, it is overwhelmingly beneficial to humanity and apparently of no proportionate bad consequences to the rest of nature. The transplantation of baboon livers to humans is a different case in many respects. The multidimensionality of values, and the consequent understanding of the different values persons or other aspects of nature or culture have for each other in different circumstances, pose very ambiguous choices in the current debates about the natural environment. Judgments about whether to use animals in biological research, as the graduate students argued about them, were basically judgments about whether

values gained and values lost were reasonably proportionate to each other. The life and death of rats compared to increments in knowledge about the neural
system is even more difficult than comparing apples and
oranges, but some comparisons have to be made to
justify either usages or nonusage. Human participation
is intentional, at least when moral issues are drawn to
our attention, and thus we are answerable for our
actions.

I have stressed that the theocentric perspective not
only provides a framework for making conscious moral
choices but also is an attitudinal, dispositional, affective stance. It is a sense of dependence, a sense of
gratitude, a sense of accountability which properly on
occasions evokes a sense of remorse and even guilt, and
a sense of the possibility to intervene for justifiable
ends. One can have these senses, and particularly a
sense of accountability, without always wallowing in a
deep sense of remorse or guilt. When I spray a wasp's
nest with the means available to me, I know I am
affecting not only the wasps but also plant life and air
around the nest. But potential dangers to my grandchildren who will play in the yard supersede those concerns. One has to compare. If I had a better way to
eliminate or at least constrain the wasps without other
harmful outcomes I would use it. But nonetheless I am

conscious of the ambiguity of the outcomes of my justifiable actions. The elimination of the wasps is a "sacrifice" which I judge to be necessary, but its gravity is not as great as the elimination of some other animal life, or human life for justifiable ends. Yet, some consciousness and feeling of even slight remorse occurs, and is salutary. It both expresses and nourishes a religious moral attitude of humility.

References and Bibliographical Notes

The quotation is from Toulmin, *The Return to Cosmology*, 255. Richard R. Niebuhr is quoted from the "Introduction" to his Neesima Lectures delivered at Doshisha University, Kyoto, Japan: *Streams of Grace: Studies in Jonathan Edwards, Samuel Taylor Coleridge and William James* (Kyoto: Doshisha University Press, 1983), 4. This particular view is drawn from William James. Hans Jonas's discussion of mobility is found in *The Phenomenon of Life: Toward a Philosophical Biology* (New York: Dell Publishing Co., 1968), 99–107, in a chapter titled "To Move and To Feel: On the Animal Soul." H. Richard Niebuhr's most concise essay on relational value theory is "The Center of Value," in *Radical Monotheism and Western Culture* (New York: Harper and Bros., 1960), 100–113; the quotation is from page 106. The second, more explicitly theological, quotation is from H. R. Niebuhr, *The Meaning of Revelation* (New York: The Macmillan Co., 1941),

167. For Fox and Swazey's article "Leaving the Field," see *Hastings Center Report* 22, no. 5 (Sept.-Oct. 1992): 9–15; the quotations are from pages 12 and 13. Leon Kass's discussion of in-vitro fertilization and its much wider implications is found in "The Meaning of Life—In the Laboratory," in *Toward a More Natural Science: Biology and Human Affairs* (New York: The Free Press, 1985), 99–127; the quotation is from page 113.

3

A Comparative Interlude
Some Religious and Theological Reflections

Much has been written comparing Eastern and Western
religious views and their different outlooks on the relations of humans to the natural environment. The late
Joseph Kitagawa gave this summary comparison:

*In contrast to the contemplation of Western peoples
meditation in the East tends to be directed toward
Sacred Reality present in Nature. This is due to the
fact that unlike their Western counterparts, who believe themselves to be situated somewhere between
God and the world of nature, Eastern people have
always accepted the humble role of being a part of
the world of nature.*

A transcendental creator-deity was never acknowledged, he avers, in the Eastern perception of a monistic

77

universe. Humans are "subservient to the regulative order or inner balance of the cosmos, variously known as *Rta, Dharma,* and *Tao.*" Bhikkhu Buddhadāsa would exemplify this in the text and anti-text of this book. I shall return to this theme later.

Of course, the theocentric perspective I have espoused is not the only Western theological and religious alternative. "Somewhere between God and the world of nature" is an area large enough for several positions, ranging from humans being despots over nature because God is so transcendent, to having dominion over nature while still being dependent on it, to being a steward of the Divine in cooperation with nature, to being subordinate to nature because Nature is God. In this chapter I shall develop a typology of the place of humans in relation to God and to nature based on the distinctions just made. While, as I have indicated in the previous chapter, participation is my choice of term, it might be worthwhile to show its relation to, both in similarities and differences, other Western alternatives. My reflections are stimulated and drawn from John Passmore's *Man's Responsibility for Nature* more than any other particular source, though many writings not cited here have informed me. Here, again, I am interested in not only beliefs about God and nature, but also the affective dispositions of persons—which may follow from beliefs or find their justification in them.

Despotism. Certainly in popular conversation God is often judged to be a despot when events for which humans cannot be held accountable are attributed to being acts of God. God freely does what God wills to do with divine power. Passmore's first chapter on the Western traditions is called "Man as Despot." The term is drawn from the political order; the despot is an absolute ruler who exercises his or her will arbitrarily and often in a tyrannical way in the service of his or her interests. There are no moral constraints upon the power that the despot uses. The despot is sovereign, has "sovereignal freedom," to cite one of Orlando Patterson's aspects of freedom in Western culture.

In this ideal-type (a mental construct for heuristic purposes and not necessarily a class into which anything fits perfectly), the natural environment can be exploited arbitrarily by humans for whatever ends they choose or perceive to be of immediate benefit to them. It is the utilitarian stance radicalized to the nth degree. No line needs to be drawn between use and abuse. Nature has no qualities of the sacred, no intrinsic rights or value. It is a mechanism. There is no significant difference between the qualities of nature and those of tools (which, of course, also can be abused as well as used) fashioned by humans to ease their labors in the world. Value is in relation to the immediate and short-range interests of those with power to determine its use—the despots.

The modern version of this type is often ascribed to Francis Bacon: "Only let the human race recover the right over nature that belongs to it by divine bequest, and let power be given it; the exercise thereof will be governed by sound reason and true religion." The quotation has more force to justify despotism if one does not read the last clause, and some citations ignore those qualifications or cite other passages that do not make them; indeed, one also remembers the end of Bacon's prayer, "to God the Father, God the Son, and God the Holy Ghost," "that knowledge being now discharged of that venom which the serpent infused into it, and which makes the mind of man to swell, we may not be wise above measure and sobriety, but cultivate truth in charity." But most striking is that the human race has "the right over nature that belongs to it by divine bequest, and let power be given it." To Bacon is attributed the modern historic attitude that science and technology provide the means for the implied right not merely to master nature sufficiently to relieve certain forms of human suffering, but to exploit nature for ends and purposes that enhance the insatiable desires of human beings for pleasure and comfort.

An earlier historical example can be found in Cicero's dialogues of *The Nature of the Gods,* in which Balbus, a Stoic, concludes his argument as follows:

The universe itself was made for both gods and men, and all that is in it was devised and ordered for the use of Man. . . . Man alone has measured out the courses of the stars and knows their times and their seasons, their changes and variety. If Man alone knows this, we must infer that it was for Man's sake that they were made. . . . What purpose do sheep serve, except from their fleeces to provide the stuff of woolen garments for mankind?

(Maybe mutton? Or a metaphor for ovine-like characteristics of some humans?) He enumerates other aspects of the natural world and claims that all exist "for the sake of Man." In other words, human activity that useing technologies of Cicero's time (e.g., irrigation) controlled and used nature for the sake of human needs and interests. Here we have a spokesman for Stoicism, so we do not have the divine bequest of the Christian Trinity, but the outcome in attitude and activity is similar.

In religious language, the human has become if not a god, at least a demigod. God has deputized humanity to be God's sovereign viceroy over nature. The position on the line "somewhere between God and the world of nature" is close to God. Human capacities to know and control nature increase, though they have not achieved the omniscience and omnipotence attributed to the Deity. What is similar between humans and God is the right to determine how power is to be exercised according to arbitrary whims. Human achievements of control and use of the natural environment are celebrated as successful use of the right, as Bacon said, that is a bequest of God. There are no internal restraints, and nature is desacralized, thingified, or in current jargon, commodified.

Has this despotism been justified theologically in the Western traditions? In my judgment, it has never completely been justified, though inferences from religious beliefs have supported moves toward it. The general idea that the entire universe was created for the sake of human beings can lend support to this type. In Thomas Aquinas the lower exists for the sake of the higher, and thus plants and animals for the benefit of humans; this follows the presumed order of perfection in which we are the most perfect created beings, next to angels. John Calvin interprets the creation narratives in Genesis to show that in the first days the earth was prepared for the coming of human beings; this and other evidences are cited to back the view that all things in nature can be put to human service. The Jewish thinkers Saadia and Maimonides are cited to be in general agreement with this view.

Among the alternating currents that passed through the wires of Protestant theology briefly in the 1960s was the celebration of secularity; the Bible's transcendent God created humanity to be free from the impediments of religiosity, that is, to be worldly or secular. Tones of optimism about technology and culture's capacities to solve many problems can be seen, among other places, in the documents of the Second Vatican Council from that decade. Despotism was not endorsed, but given other conditions than religious beliefs, moves toward that ideal-type could occur with the approval of many people.

Has there been criticism of the tendency to this type in Western religion? Certainly there has. For example, although Martin Buber did not address the status of the natural environment as a special problem in his religious thought, his interpretation of human life in relation to God and nature had a powerful prophetic edge. The distinction between I-Thou and I-It relations gets to the point. Nature can be an It, and human beings

83

can be Its; anything existing can be an It. "The primary relation of man to the world of It is comprised of *experiencing,* which continually constitutes the world, and *using,* which leads the world to its manifold aim, the sustaining, relieving, and equipping of human life." This seems no different from the manifold aim of the lower forms of life existing for the service of humans. Using the world as an It, relating to it as an It (including the natural environment) is necessary for human life.

But to relate to others, including the natural environment, also as a *Thou* is to relate to them as "compassed in an eternal *Thou,*" even though the eternal *Thou* (God) "is not compassed" in nature. In relating to others in I-Thou rather than I-It relations "we look out toward the fringe of the eternal *Thou;*" "we are aware of the breath from the eternal *Thou,*" God. God can use as a vessel of God's word, as a place of God's meeting, human beings, "an animal, a plant, a stone."

As I noted, Buber's writings adduced here do not have an ecological crisis particularly in mind. They have a deeper kind of prophetic message to the human community, a more inclusive one. When other persons and nature and its parts are "thingified," related to only as Its for their utility value, there is a diminishment not only of the other but also of human lives. The sense of life as Spirit, the sense of the world as a vessel through which persons relate to God and God to persons begins to evaporate. The mystery of life is lost. Despotism is a maximal I-It relation to the natural environment. While human relations to the natural environment necessarily swing between "itness" and "Thouness," nature cannot be reduced to *It*. To be related to nature as *Thou,* as a realm of Spirit, both as a way of thinking about it and sensing it, precludes an authorization of despotism. But relating to nature as *It* is also necessary.

Probably the most common and sharpest theological criticism of a tendency to human despotism over the natural environment is that despots, whether dealing with communities or nature, have usurped the divine prerogatives, especially if God is understood to be omniscient and omnipotent and to have a kind of arbitrary will. Put plainly, despotism is idolatry. Human interests and desires become sovereign. They deny both dependence upon powers beyond their control and claim sovereignal freedom over the powers that are in their control. Explication and defense of the charge of idolatry can be made in purely theological terms: God is God and humans are creatures, therefore not God. Thus it is theologically wrong for humans to assume that they have the capacities of God and thus to usurp despotic power. Of course, any theology which posits an utterly

85

capricious, arbitrary god has not had significant support in the Western traditions.

One need not take recourse to theological arguments against despotism, for practical purposes. As I indicated in the second chapter, on the basis of undesirable outcomes of such an attitude and practices, the threats to humans, to biodiversity, and so on, are sufficient to avoid despotism. Each of the "centrisms" I described there, however, has correlates in its objects of valuation and loyalty, which is to say in its functional equivalents of theological and religious beliefs and outlooks. Each has its own idolatrous tendencies. Luther's *Larger Catechism,* in the exposition of the first commandment, says that "the trust and faith of the heart alone make both God and an idol." The center of human valuation, which often strongly determines attitudes and actions, functions as a god. In despotism, humans then function as a god, or as the absolute viceroys of God; this is to have misplaced confidence which leads to devastating consequences for humans and the natural environment. It does not take seriously human finitude, our limits of knowledge, foreknowledge, and power to control all outcomes of human actions. The root of the human fault is, as I argued in *Ethics from a Theocentric Perspective,* contraction of our thinking and our affections, of our loyalties and concerns. Despotism is the extreme form of anthropocentrism; it claims human self-sufficiency.

Dominion. This type is situated "somewhere between God and the world of nature," further from God than despotism, but closer than stewardship. The classical source in Judaism and Christianity for the idea of human dominion over nature is found in Genesis 1:26: "Then God said, Let us make man in our image and likeness to rule the fish in the sea, the birds in the heaven, the cattle, all wild animals on earth, and all reptiles that crawl upon the earth." Some have argued, and others rebutted, that this verse of the Bible is responsible for what has come to be a despotic attitude of man toward nature. The historian Lynn White's article in *Science* in 1967 had deep and wide influence because of its indictment of biblical religions precisely on this point. The roots of the ecological crisis are religious, according to White. He writes that the problems derive from "Christian attitudes towards man's relation to nature which are almost universally held not only by Christians and neo-Christians but also by those who fondly regard themselves as post-Christians," namely those attitudes that make us view ourselves as "superior to nature, contemptuous of it, willing to use it for our slightest whim." Dominion, here, really is despotism.

As I have noted, both historical and contemporary

evidence can be cited to show that Western religion has justified a kind of despotism on the basis of the biblical idea of human dominion over nature. One general argument that has been cited is the interpretation of those passages of Jewish scriptures in which the religion of Israel differentiated itself from the nature religion of the Canaanites with its gods of fertility. One can find passages in modern Christian theology that argue that the arena of Yahweh's action for the true religious community is history and not nature. The theology of secularization in the 1960s' technology was celebrated partly on the grounds that for Christians nature has no inherent sacred qualities; thus it may be used by humans to fulfill their aspirations. The book that made Harvey Cox famous, *The Secular City,* was interpreted by many readers and critics as celebrating a secularization of the "world" grounded in a biblical theology, and thus a celebration of technology's triumphs over nature. And also in some support of White's argument general comparisons like Kitagawa's were made by many authors between Christianity and Judaism on the one hand and Buddhism and Hinduism on the other to the point that a certain sacrality imputed to nature in those Eastern religions has led historically to more reverence for nature than is the case in the West. For some observers, the two Western religious persons who could provide some counterevidence to White's thesis are St. Francis and Albert Schweitzer.

Religious writers who take the idea of *dominion* seriously but avoid its possible despotic tendencies often point to wider religious and theological dimensions that White and others are charged with ignoring. They admit, necessarily, the anthropocentrism that one finds in such writers as Thomas Aquinas and John Calvin, but believe it is qualified significantly in their wider theological contexts. William C. French, for example, has argued that the Thomistic idea of natural law provides a basis for interpreting the human always in relation to the whole of creation, that a kind of interdependence of human life with the rest of nature is there in Aquinas, and that Catholicism can retrieve from its great medieval theology a basis for an ethics of respect for nature, and even for the intrinsic value of nature based upon its creation by God who created all things "good." He argues that one can have a "Creation-centered paradigm rather than a human subject-centered paradigm within Roman Catholic theology."

Karl Barth wrote with assurance that

God is obviously not interested in the totality of things and beings created by Him, not in specific beings within this totality, but in man, in this being, who in his distinctive unity of soul and body is in his

*own time alive through his spirit, in his individuality
and freedom and with his orientation on God and
solidarity with his kind.*

Life is to be affirmed, but it "is no second God, and
therefore the respect due to it cannot rival the reverence owed to God." Does this mean for Barth that
dominion should take the direction of despotism? I
think not. He wrote that

*the world of animals and plants forms the indispens-
able living background to the living-space divinely al-
lotted to man and placed under his control. As they
live, so can he. He is not set up as lord over the
earth, but as lord on the earth which is already fur-
nished with these creatures. Animals and plants do
not belong to him; they and the whole earth can belong only to God.*

Despotism assumes sovereign ownership and thus implies the right to use nature arbitrarily; dominion for
Barth is based on life as a "loan" of something belong-
ing to God, and thus respect is due to nonhuman life.
He distinguished between our relations to plants and
animals; plants can be harvested but the killing of
an animal is its annihilation. "And the nearness of
the animal to man irrevocably means that when man

kills a beast he does something which is very similar to homicide." Thus Barth distinguishes between "reverence of life," as Albert Schweitzer proposed, and "respect for life." The former in Barth's view is a kind of nature mysticism that does not make proper differentiations; respect means that one can use nature for human well-being but that to do so is "a priestly act," a kind of sacrificial act of great moral and religious importance. Nature is not sacred but a gift of God.

Martin Buber's view could also support dominion. While it avoids the sacralization of nature one finds in the subordination type, its view of the ultimate Thou, and of Spirit, infuses an aura of mystery to human experience that Barth's view eschews. But, like Barth's, it recognizes the appropriateness of the use of nature, an *It* relation to nature, for human life and activity.

Dominion recognizes the natural environment and all of life as a gift from the goodness of God. God created all things and saw that they were good, indeed, very good. In this religious context receiving a gift evokes not only gratitude for it but also a sense of responsibility for its care and use. One can note the difference of this relation in the contexts of religion and law. In positive law a gift is a gift; there are no strings of responsibility attached for how it is to be used. One can also note that in many recent discussions of the gift relationship, for example, between the recipient and donor of a human organ, there seems to be a natural human accenting of the sense of dependency on the part of the recipient, and in some cases a kind of continuing sense of proprietary interest on the part of the giver. Indeed, the language of God "owning" the world can be found in theological literature. While human agency and capacities are acknowledged to determine the use of what is given, the human does not have a quit-claim deed to the environment. This leads to my third type, stewardship.

Stewardship. The ideal-type of dominion can move in one direction toward despotism if some of its features are exaggerated; it also moves in another direction toward stewardship. Stewardship, I believe, has been the most preferred way of understanding man's responsibilities for nature in Judaism and Christianity. The steward is a caretaker of what he or she does not own. The caretaker is responsible to God who is the "owner" or the giver of all that is. Karl Barth who uses the idea of gift also says that all life is a loan to humankind. Presumably what is loaned to one has to be returned in at least as good condition as it was when the loan was made. Another way of phrasing the grounds for stewardship is that the gift of life given ultimately by God not only requires that humans ought to be thankful for

92

it, but also entails obligations to care for the gift, to respect it and not to treat it wantonly. The *dominion*, the ultimate power and authority, is retained by God; humans are the stewards of God's purposes and rule in life. Other terms similar to stewardship have been used: humans are God's *deputies* who are charged with the conduct of affairs (in our case the use of nature) in accord with God's purposes; or humans are *agents* of God and thus do not have final authority but are authorized by God to act on God's behalf in the conduct of life in the world.

I illustrate this ideal-type from the work of Douglas John Hall of McGill University in Montreal. The subtitle of Hall's book *Imaging God* is *Dominion as Stewardship*. To make his argument, Hall interprets Genesis 1:26 on humans being made in the image and likeness of God in what he believes to be a novel way. He argues that the traditional view of that passage "baptized" certain endowments of power and authority in human beings that were like the power and authority attributed to God. This led to praising whatever endowments and powers—such as rationality and freedom—of the human were dominant in a given culture. In ours, it leads to a kind of despotic attitude toward nature. In contrast with this Hall proposes what he calls a "relational" view of the idea of the image of God in humans. The intention of this conception "is to position the human crea-ture responsibly in relation to other creatures; not to demonstrate that this creature is higher, or more com-plex, or worthier, but to designate a specific function of this creature—a very positive function—in relation to others. Relationship is of the essence of this creature's nature and vocation." This is worked out in terms of humans "being-with" other creatures and with aspects of nature as well as being-with God. Humans are re-sponsive to other creatures and bear responsibility for them.

This view, in Hall's judgment, would transform the human attitude and outlook toward the natural envi-ronment; humans would be both identified with it and differentiated from it, but the idea of "communion" with nature (as presumably there is communion with God) would lead to sounder policies and actions in the ecological circumstances of life. One notes that Hall's book, like some others, is provoked by the perception of an ecological crisis and thus is an effort to reinterpret mainstream "biblical theology" in such a way that a new interpretation supports ecologically sound policies. Thus dominion becomes stewardship as human life and activity are reconceived relationally: relationally with reference both to God and to the natural world.

The ideal-type of stewardship does not sacralize nature; it is not a nature mysticism in the sense of Schweitzer's "reverence for life." The relation of the Deity to nature differs in various authors whose writings are illumined by this ideal-type. Some come quite close to nature mysticism: the immanent presence of God is in nature, or at least in ordering nature, but nature is not God. Others are farther from nature mysticism: Nature is a gift of God and thus we treat it like we would a cherished gift from a good parent or a good friend. Its "goodness" in providing conditions for life on earth gives it a status requiring respect different from the status it has in the despotic attitude, and does not permit the ideal of *dominion* to move in that direction. Stewardship moves toward participation in nature which I turn to after discussing subordination.

Subordination. On the spectrum that Kitagawa suggests, subordination is the characteristic Eastern religious position; it is the opposite of despotism. As an ideal-type in a very pure form it is seldom found in the Western religious tradition and perhaps not in any religious tradition at all. That extreme type would militate against any human intervention in nature; what the type usually helps us to see is something like Bhikkhu Buddhadāsa's affirmation that "anything which exists

95

in a proper condition is in equilibrium with everything else." Even the hunter-gatherers intervened in the natural environment in order to establish conditions necessary for their survival and their way of life. Early in the development of our species came the use of plants and the beginnings of agriculture. The Genesis creation narratives differentiate between Abel as a shepherd and Cain as a tiller of soil. Building shelters, using clothing, and developing herbal medicines are only some examples of human activities that defy utter subordination to the natural environment. Humans develop cultures, and cultures always use or affect nature in unintended ways.

I have already noted the difficulties in establishing what an equilibrium would be. If it suggests harmony between humans and the environment, where is the score and who has written it? If it suggests cooperation, the way is open for interventions which presumably avoid conflict, but it is difficult to illustrate any that are not destructive of some aspect of the environment. Recall my illustrations of how aspects of the natural environment conflict with each other.

When Calvin assured his readers that they could say that "Nature is God" provided it was said with a reverent heart, he did not forget to add that one ought not confuse the works of God with God. Because he could interpret particular natural events as fulfilling divine purposes, such as the lactation that begins when a mother has given birth, he had also to interpret unfortunate outcomes of natural processes, such as some mothers not lactating sufficiently, as somehow within the divine purposes. I call this to attention to show that "Nature is God" (or at least God acting purposively for humans in natural processes) can be used to interpret the meanings of very specific events. How one would interpret the divine intention or determination in specific natural processes and events depends, obviously, on the judgments made about what God's intentions are for humans and their environment. When metaphors, such as the earth as "God's body" are used, their implications for human activity depend, likewise, on what is claimed about the divine intentions.

Coming closest to an ideal-type of subordination in Western religious literature is the work of Albert Schweitzer, as I have indicated earlier. He wrote,

Ethics alone can put me in true relationship with the Universe by my serving it, cooperating with it; not by trying to understand it. . . . Only by serving every kind of life do I enter the service of the Creative Will whence all life emanates. I do not understand

*it; but I do know (and it is sufficient to live by) that
by serving life, I serve the Creative Will. This is the
mystical significance of ethics.*

Elsewhere Schweitzer argues that the ethics of reverence for life makes no distinctions between higher
and lower, what is more or less precious as forms of life.
To do this, he argues, is to establish standards of grada-
tion that are always in relation to ourselves as humans,
judging values by what is closest to us and more distant
from us. He can ask how we could possibly know, when
we value life in relation to ourselves only, the importance of organisms in themselves and in terms of the
universe of which they are a part.

Although few current writers draw from Schweitzer,
many resonate with this ethics of mysticism in one way
or another. For example, is the natural world of intrinsic value and not simply instrumental value with reference to humans, or even with reference to other aspects
of nature? This question is much addressed, as I have
shown. Those who do write in a vein similar to
Schweitzer do not always add the religious dimension
that he has, and if they do, it is not always in his terms
of the Creative Will as the source of the will to live in
all nature. It may be the sense of wonder that Konner
writes about, or biophilia, as E. O. Wilson describes.

None of these imply subordination, but they point to a respect for the otherness of the natural world, something beyond human capacities to create upon which we are dependent, and thus evokes, if not Schweitzer's reverence, at least profound respect.

Participation in nature. This is the ideal-type which sheds most light on my interpretation of the place of the human between God and the natural world. It coheres with the theocentric perspective; it is not a deduction from the idea of God, but one of its sources. I have introduced it earlier, and develop it more here.

The premises of this type are not derived from traditional, biblical sources as are those of dominion and stewardship. Rather they are derived from observations about all life in the world that are backed by modern sciences. The text from Bhikkhu Buddhadāsa is appropriate: "Nothing exists independently; everything exists interdependently." It fits the relational theory of value developed in the second chapter. Human beings participate in the patterns and processes of interdependence of life in the world. All life, including human, is dependent upon these processes and patterns. In cosmological terms, granting differences among accounts, and in evolutionary terms, this is the case. We and the natural environment we inhabit would not have come to be apart from aeons of development in the cosmos, in the development of life on our planet, in the development of mammalian species, etc. If current hypotheses about the vast destruction of dinosaurs due to the earth being hit by a large meteor are accurate, very powerful natural events have determined the course of the development of life. And we continue to be dependent upon these patterns and processes, as various threats to them inform us if nothing else does—for example, the possible greenhouse effects, shifting tectonic plates, volcanic eruptions both under the sea and on the land, the meteorological effects of "el niño," hurricanes and tornados, and lesser storms. We are conscious of this dependence when we reflect upon not only the sustaining powers of weather, earth, plants, and animals, but also when we see the conditions for sustenance threatened by soil erosion, by the use of chemicals that find their way into the air or seep through soil to water supplies, and by excessive human population growth. Even our most primal observations of the natural world are affected by human participation; those of us who live in large urban centers that are artificially lighted never see the stars as one does from the high country in Wyoming on a clear night. The visual effect of urban life subtly makes us less conscious of the minuscule bit of the cosmos we inhabit.

Religious dimensions of dim or articulate senses of

dependence on the environment and interdependence with it, a sense of the contingency of our lives and the natural world relative to our powers to control them, are probably present in all the world's religions, on a continuum from those that have been called animistic to the most radical views of divine transcendence. They are also found in the natural piety I have noted to be present in many secular persons as well. We did not create the fundamental conditions out of which life emerged, the necessary conditions for animal life and finally human life to develop; we do not create ourselves (even in-vitro fertilization is a technology which manipulates ova and sperm to enable an embryo to come into being); we have not determined our own fundamental genetic endowments; we are mortal and bound to die, though our dying can be prolonged by medical technology; we cannot fully control our individual destinies but are subject to constraints and possibilities objective to ourselves. All this evokes profound religious, affective sensibilities.

In the Genesis account Cain and Abel participated in nature, Cain by tilling and Abel by caring for flocks that grazed. The fourth chapter of Genesis goes on to tell readers that Cain was a builder of cities, that other descendants of Adam lived in tents, played the harp and the pipe, and were coppersmiths and blacksmiths.

Thus the development of cultures and technologies through human participation in nature is noted in our biblical myths. It is commonplace, but nonetheless true, that especially in modern technological societies (and modern technology penetrates increasingly all societies) that our participation increasingly affects the natural environment and the qualities of human life and action. Among many authors who have attempted to make us conscious of this staggeringly novel condition is the late Hans Jonas in *The Imperative of Responsibility*. Many effects of our participation are incremental, and we really do not sense the long-range significance of their outcomes. They are often destructive to other things while they benefit humans. And our reliance on them, some observe, is itself gradually "dehumanizing" in the sense that outcomes of the efficient cause of technologies and their success intervenes between us and our continuing inexorable ultimate dependence on nature. We become, some argue, less human as we become "denatured," that is, more and more products of a technologically constructed world.

These matters have been explicated in terms of relational value theory in the previous chapter. They cohere with the theocentric perspective, with a view of the Divine as the ultimate power in "whose hands" (to resort to anthropomorphism) is the destiny of all things and the ultimate source of all human good, but does not guarantee it. Indeed, that power and those powers that order life manifest functionally interdependent relations that threaten human good and cannot be excessively violated without destroying what we deem to be good for us, who are only a part of what is empowered and ordered by God through nature.

To sum up, human beings participate in the patterns and processes of interdependence of life in the world. We can and should intervene for the sake of humans and nature itself. Our participation is a response to events and conditions in which we live; it involves valuing aspects of nature in relation not only to our own interests but also the "interests" of other aspects of nature. Human life is dependent not only upon the processes and patterns of nature, but also upon human intentional participation in them for the sake of survival and other justifiable values to the human species, communities and individuals. It takes seriously our biological histories; we have come to be as a result of processes of nature in the cosmos, in the development of this planet, and the development of mammalian species, etc. And we continue to be dependent on these processes and patterns, learning to avoid threats our interventions create to the well-being of the human and all living things and to consent to the limits of our control when we see volcanic eruptions and hurricanes and tornadoes and earthquakes.

The religious dimensions are those described at the end of the first chapter: the awe, the sublime, the sense of limits as well as possibilities. The responsibilities we have are vastly increased with the development of culture and technologies that can enhance human values by relief of suffering and development of arts, as well as perception of evils, the *malum,* as Hans Jonas has argued. Outcomes of our participation are usually incremental in both their beneficial and destructive forms, though the possibilities of catastrophic outcomes lurk in the existence of nuclear weapons and the greenhouse effect.

In this view we look to an ordering of nature as one basis, but not a sufficient one, for deciding what goods for whom, and for what, ought to be pursued. This basis for ethics is informed by sciences, ecology in particular, but also by human experience as we confront the adverse effects of our interventions. But choices have to take account of contexts; the values are always in relation to them. Ethics worked out with reference to acid rain are in their particularities different from those worked out with reference to using nuclear weapons, cutting timber in North America or Asia, or disposing of waste in large metropolitan areas. Population growth, the successful effects of capacities to increase life spans but unsuccessful effects of limits to births, is one of the most glaring practical problems emerging from our participation in nature. Underlying whatever policies we choose, whatever personal choices we make about consumption, is an ordering of nature, not in perfect static equilibrium, but in a dynamism of interdependencies that warns us of limitations and awakens us to threats to human well-being as well as to the biodiversity of life itself. The theological correlate is a Deity whose ultimate power working through the interdependencies of life makes possible human well-being and the well-being of other things, but a Deity that does not guarantee the human good.

The little boy in My Life as a Dog kept saying, "One has to compare." In his case it was his own suffering in relation to that dog in a sputnik, revolving around and around the earth. In our case it is that the multidimensionality of values in everything is actualized in the relations of beings or things to each other. We work out some provisional priorities, but many choices based on them are somewhat morally ambiguous, costing the values of some relations to benefit from others. And the choices are context-related. But lurking in, through, under, and above the choices is the difficult issue of how the parts we value in specific relations are related to the value of the whole, the whole of nature and our part in it, and how what is good for the whole is related to the parts. We might idealize a world in which the values in particular relations work harmoniously for the good of the whole; we might eschatologize this, looking toward some coming or eternal kingdom in which this harmony will be realized. But, I believe, it is not ours to know such things. Even a complete set of priorities cannot be perfectly hierarchical, so that there is one set of value relations that in every circumstance trumps all others. Only the most extreme utilitarian view and most extreme intrinsic value view can be absolutely consistent. We are in a situation that calls for respect for nature, but not a Schweitzerian reverence. Perhaps in a very general way the following imperative can direct us: "Act so that you consider all things never *only* as a means to your ends, or even to collective human ends."

But what concepts, vocabularies, and theories do we use in making personal and policy choices? In the fourth chapter we will examine, but hardly resolve, the disciplinary cacophony of policy discussion.

References and Bibliographical Notes

The comparison of Eastern and Western religion is from Joseph M. Kitagawa's collection of essays, *The History of Religions: Understanding Human Experience* (Atlanta: Scholars Press, 1987), 246. John Passmore, *Man's Responsibility for Nature: Ecological Problems and Western Traditions* (New York: Scribners, 1974), covers much the same literature as Glacken's book but in a briefer and more thematic way. Orlando Patterson, in his interpretation of the idea of freedom in Western culture (*Freedom,* vol. 1 [New York: Basic Books, 1991]), distinguishes three aspects (or types) of the idea: sovereignal, civic, and personal (pp. 3–4 and throughout). The first Francis Bacon quotation is from Aphorism 129, *Novum Organum,* in E. A. Burtt, ed., *The English Philosophers from Bacon to Mill* (New York: Random House Modern Library, 1939), 86. Bacon's prayer is from *The Great Instauration,* in Burtt, ed., 12. The Cicero quotations are excerpted from *The Nature of the Gods* (New York: Penguin Books, 1972), 185–89. One of many sources for Thomas Aquinas's description of the hierarchy of beings is *Summa Theologiae,* 1a, q.47 ("On the Distinction of Things in General"). One relevant passage from Calvin is *The Institutes,* 1, 14,2, in McNeill, ed., 1: 161–62. Passmore quotes passages from Saadia and Maimonides on page 12; Glacken offers a more qualified interpretation of Maimonides (222–24). All but the last quotation are from Buber, *I and Thou* (Edinburgh: T. and T. Clark, 1937), 38, 6, and 101; the last is from Buber, *Between Man and Man* (London: Routledge and Kegan Paul, 1947), 10. Among various publications of Luther's *Larger*

Catechism, see T. G. Tappert, ed., *The Book of Concord* (Philadelphia: Muhlenberg Press, 1959); the quotation is from page 365. My discussion of sin as "contraction" is in *Ethics from a Theocentric Perspective* 1: 293–306. White's article, "The Historical Roots of Our Ecology Crisis," has achieved almost canonical status in discussions of religion and ecology; most authors, including me, cite it as a point of departure. It was first published in *Science* 155 (1967): 1203–1207; the quotation is from page 1204. At least one critic interpreted Cox, *The Secular City* (New York: Macmillan, 1990), to represent the "Christ of Culture" type in H. R. Niebuhr's *Christ and Culture* (New York: Harper and Bros., 1951). William French continues to work with this theme; the citation here is from "Subject-centered and Creation-centered Paradigms in Recent Catholic Thought," *Journal of Religion* 70 (1990): 48–72.

All the quotations from Barth are to be found in Section 55 of *Church Dogmatics,* which is headed as follows: "As God the Creator calls man to Himself and turns him to his fellowman, He orders him to honour his own life and that of every other man as a loan, and to secure it against all caprice, in order that it may be used in this service and in preparation for this service"; *Church Dogmatics,* III/4 (Edinburgh: T. and T. Clark, 1961), 324. The quotations are from the first subsection, "Respect for Life," 337, 342, 351, 352, and 355. See Douglas John Hall, *Imaging God: Dominion as Stewardship* (Grand Rapids: Eerdmans Publishing Co., 1986); quotation is from pages 106–7. Many other books by theologians and religious leaders could be cited to support the notion that the ideal-type of stewardship is very strong, if not dominant in recent Christian writings. For some people it is still too human-centered; it supports too much human autonomy. Readers are referred to the bibliography in McDaniel, *Of God and Pelicans* if they wish to explore more of this literature.

Calvin's observations about lactation are found in *The Institutes,* 1, 16, 3, in McNeill, ed., 1: 200–201. The quotation is from Schweitzer's famous essay, "The Ethics of Reverence for Life," which can be found in Henry Clark, *The Ethical Mysticism of Albert Schweitzer* (Boston: Beacon Press, 1962), 189. N. Katherine Hayles, at the end of her cultural studies account of sciences and literature, writes about "denaturing" texts, language, contexts, time, and the human as a result of the logic of postmodernism. On the latter her example is Donna Haraway's "cyborgs." See Hayles, *Chaos Bound* (Ithaca, N.Y.: Cornell University Press, 1990), 265–95, especially pp. 292–95. The concluding sentence is from my *Ethics from a Theocentric Perspective* 2: 135.

4

Disciplinary Arcs
Can the Circle Be Closed?

I referred earlier to a recent book, *Ecology, Economics, Ethics: The Broken Circle*. The circle is hard to close, not only between these three disciplines, but because politics, state and local law, regulations, and international law are also among its arcs.

While the cold war was still going on, Robert Sachs, a physicist, and I conducted a seminar on "Ethics and Nuclear Deterrence" for faculty members from various institutions in the Chicago area for about three years. We had participants from relevant disciplines: philosophy, theology, physics, international relations, Soviet studies, military strategy, law, and even rhetoric. Although the seminar elicited some papers that were published with others in an issue of the journal *Ethics*, it was finally discontinued because of our failure to close the circle between the perspectives, modes of analysis, conceptual frameworks, and modes of argument that were represented. Huge and important problems like nuclear war or the environmental crisis are relevant to many academic disciplines, but the specialization of disciplines makes it extraordinarily difficult to come to an agreement on policy recommendations.

Which discipline, with its concepts and modes of analysis and argument, ought to be central, ought to bring the others into its orbit? Our last seminar paper was by a moral philosopher who argued cogently from a basically Kantian frame of reference that if it is immoral to use nuclear weapons it is immoral to threaten to use them. From the perspectives of the military and political disciplines this argument was totally out of touch with the realities of the European political and military situation at that time. The philosopher began with ethics and stayed with ethics; other colleagues wanted to begin with political and military analysis of the circumstances. The circle, in that high-powered group, could not be closed.

When we examine environmental issues, at least as many academic disciplines pertain as they did in discussions of nuclear arms control. The world in which choices are made and actions are taken is not conveniently divisible by our academic specializations. The multidimensionality of any way we conceive the environmental problem becomes clear when we ask what sorts of information we need, what forms of analysis are appropriate, which concepts are proper to use, and what modes of arguments are most persuasive in proposing some solutions. And when we propose solutions, whether they pertain to our individual conduct, or to whether a dam ought to be built on the Delaware River, whether the spotted owl takes preference over lumbering, or how the use of chlorofluorocarbons (CFCs) should be controlled all over the world, the conflicts are not only about means but also about values or ends. Nature is a multidimensional source of values, and its values are specified in relation to other things, other values that we cherish. There is not a harmony. Remember my Thai monk: everything exists interdependently. But also remember my dissent: there is tension rather than equilibrium.

Academics necessarily opt for one discipline to be more adequate as a source of information, modes of analysis, or concepts, than are other disciplines. The economist sees, for example, market forces as the most determinative in the development of something perceived to be a problem, and quite reasonably sees market forces to be the principal means for the resolution. Thus proposals are being formed to "sell" pollution rights. The demographer might see human population growth as the most significant factor in the depletion of nature, and thus high on that list of solutions is population control, voluntary, one hopes, or coerced, as in China. A theologian might see the insatiability of self-interested desires, sin, as the principal, or one of the principal, causes of environmental depletion, and argue either for radical conversion of attitudes and actions or for restraints that require some measure of coercion. A political scientist is especially skilled at weighing the political implications of any proposed solution and recognizes the possibilities and impediments for effective legislation or regulation. A historian of culture might trace shifting attitudes toward nature present not only in writings that address nature particularly, but also in visual arts, poetry, and other forms of literature. The biologist will focus on the importance of biodiversity for sustaining of all life as well as the conditions to further evolution of forms of life.

It is no wonder that colleges and universities are establishing courses in environmental studies that are interdisciplinary in character, whether taught by one person or by several, or that institutes are established to attempt to bring the contributions of various disciplines to bear on the issues.

Every effort to define an environmental issue itself

reflects selection factors. *Preserving the Global Environment,* edited by Jessica Tuchman Mathews, to which I shall return, chose the global environment; this is supported by evidence that the problem is global and thus the solutions involve international treaties, regulations, economics, and so on. A 1976 book, *When Values Conflict: Essays on Environmental Analysis, Discourse and Decision,* focuses on a proposal to build a dam on the Delaware River and is almost as complex as the focus on the use of CFCs. I have a poster from Bill McKibben, for whom consumerism is a major factor, that shows various ways to have an environmentally sound Christmas holiday, suggesting that gifts be wrapped in old wallpaper or pieces of fabric, that sunflower seeds be put out on Christmas Day so the birds can also celebrate, and that the total of gift-giving be limited to one hundred dollars. What various disciplines or activists define as an issue depends not only upon their science or other academic discipline, but also on the ends and means by which their specific focus can be affected by policy or action.

I shall do better at demonstrating the problem of tensions among disciplines than resolving it in this chapter. As a way to demonstrate it I shall focus attention on two recent books, *Loving Nature: Ecological Integrity and Christian Responsibility,* by James A. Nash, and *Preserving the Global Environment*, edited by Jessica Tuchman Mathews.

Among various theological approaches to ethics and human problems, Nash has chosen the idea of love as the principal point of departure and guiding outlook for considering the environmental issues. In a sense, the question is this: What does love require of responsible persons when they consider both policy and personal choices that affect the environment? It is somewhat unfair simply to list the propositions about politics that are his conclusions, since he embellishes them and shows applicability in more detail than the propositions suggest. But the propositions are what in the early years of my career were called "middle axioms." That is, from the principle of love one infers axioms that are not necessarily logical entailments of the principle of love, but are reasonable inferences drawn from it with reference to the social issue under examination. The axioms, however, are not *sufficient* to settle tensions among disciplines relevant to policy or resolve policy choices.

Nash's middle axioms are as follows:

1. "An ecologically sound and morally responsible public policy must continually resolve the economics-ecology dilemma."

2. "[It] will include public regulations that are sufficient to match social and ecological needs."

3. "[It] will protect the interests of future generations."

4. "[It] will provide protection for nonhuman species, ensuring the conditions necessary for their perpetuation and ongoing evolution."

5. "[It] will promote international cooperation as an essential means to confront the global ecological crisis."

6. "[It] will pursue ecological integrity in intimate alliance with the struggle for social peace and justice."

Each of these "axioms" indicates an objective that Nash supports on the basis of Christian love, but others could support from other background beliefs or convictions. Each of them indicates desirable outcomes in general. All of us probably agree with them, though we might disagree on what policies or actions are best to achieve them.

One can interpret each axiom to exclude certain objectives: (1) ecological policy should *not* be resolved on the basis of economic efficiency alone; (2) it should *not* leave everything to voluntary restraints or to free market forces but use regulations; (3) it should *not* limit itself to the interests of our generation; (4) it should *not* view all other species simply as potentially beneficial to human interests; (5) it should *not* be pursued in the interest of national goals alone and it should *not* be pursued without consideration of the impact on social peace and justice. This interpretation suggests that they set the boundaries beyond which it would be morally impermissible to develop policy. Or, the axioms in either the positive or negative form are points to be considered in making policy choices that involve many other considerations as well.

A strength of Nash's book is its appeal to a particular community, the Christian community, which adheres to beliefs about God known through the biblical accounts, and about the human responses and actions that properly respond to the God of love. The middle axioms, as I noted, can be sustained on other belief conditions; Nash makes the case that Christians ought to direct their personal and policy choices under their guidance. His is, of course, not the only possible Christian ethical approach, but is characteristic of much Protestant social ethics.

Attention to Nash provokes a caesura in this chapter to consider why different approaches to ecological ethics can, or ought to be, grounded in particular historic religious traditions. The morphology of Nash's argument can be interpreted in the following way. God is love, and God loves what God has created. Christians in response to the indicative of God's love have an imperative to love not only other persons but also nature. The appeal is to basic religious convictions, to the theology and articulates them, and to the experience that confirms them. In a similar way, Bhikkhu Buddhadāsa's belief in *dhamma,* articulated in the interdependence of all things, implied for him that anything that is in proper condition will be in equilibrium with everything else. On the basis of this, both attitudes and actions in the natural environment should follow. The ends, in both cases, are of universal significance; the beliefs, attitudes, and experiences that motivate and direct action are historically particular.

This interpretation sees the authority of the belief conditions to be represented in specific traditions, whether a universal truth claim is made for those beliefs or not. The imperative that follows is hypothetical; if one holds these beliefs, then one ought to have the attitudes and engage in the actions and policies that follow. This is one way that particular traditions are related to admonished or prescribed moral outlooks and activities. The Christian, or the Buddhist, tradition is the "story of the life" of those people; it is their distinctive access to understanding the relations of the ultimate reality to the particularities of nature. A "confessional" theology and ethics follows that may or may not claim that the tradition is the only access to understanding these relations.

A stronger claim might be made in the Christian tradition, namely that God has chosen to be revealed only in, let us say, the Bible and Christian tradition. From such a position authors will strive to show that the resulting theology provides a privileged and largely sufficient basis for our actions in the natural world. The particular starting point claims universal and exclusive validity for its distinctiveness, and efforts are made to find themes, passages, and symbols from the Bible to warrant ecological ethics. Such a view can be painfully offensive, and should be so in the eyes of some of its adherents, to persons who do not share the view of biblical revelation. It can also appear to be painfully defensive; it might suggest that sustaining a view of biblical authority is more important than its contribution to ecological ethics.

A third and slightly different position can be taken. The identity of the tradition itself is at stake when ecological ethics is based upon some vague Emersonian, or currently equivalent, sense of the presence of the spirit, or the divine, in nature. For the sake of maintaining a community with the revelatory powers of its central figure and its concepts and symbols for the interpretation of human life in the world, it is necessary to show how those concepts and symbols, and how the faith and loyalty to that community, are relevant to issues of ecological ethics. If this position is articulated, the purpose of preserving particular religious identity is primary over the contribution it makes to current ecological issues.

Distinguishable from each of these is the use of a particular religious tradition for the religious and moral insight it provides for our interpretation of the relations of God to the world and to public discourse about ecological issues. No claims need to be made for exclusivity or for sufficiency as a basis for ecological ethics while indicating the value of its contributions. One judgment would be on that value, rather than the authority of the tradition from which the value comes. Warrants can be made for revision of some of the tenets of the tradition on various grounds including rather critical analyses of the ways in which some tenets have sustained the extreme utilitarian views of nature for the benefits of the human. New metaphors can be stated and defined, or old ones revised, which are heterodox in the eyes of more traditionalistic members of the

121

Christian community. How radical the revisions are will affect the reception of such views in the churches. The center of belief and fidelity can be stated theologically, as it is in the theocentric perspective of this book, and argued for in terms other than the insight it yields, while demonstrating that such insight and relevant attitudes follow from it.

End of caesura; I return to the main line of analysis of this chapter.

Jessica Tuchman Mathews's edited volume of papers, *Preserving the Global Environment,* provides a sharp contrast to Nash's Christian ethical approach. Also, these papers are devoid of any appeal to the sense of the sublime. There is a shared concern, indicated by the title, but each author addresses it from the disciplinary perspective that informs his or her contributions to policy. Like all persons who begin with the inquiry, "What is going on?" these authors have to propose analyses of the principal causal factors that create the problem to be addressed. Is it unrestrained human population growth? Is it pollution resulting from technology? Is it depletion of forests and soil? Is it the insatiability of human desires? Is it the absence of authorized power to legislate or regulate activity so that the values of environment are not depleted? Is it all of the above?

If one factor could be agreed upon as the primary cause, then one could select the most appropriate discipline and propose policies which would effectively alter it, including the means for their enforcement. If, as is clear from the Mathews book and many others, there are multiple interacting causal factors, then any policy proposals have to be inclusive enough to affect each and their interactions, and relevant disciplines intersect.

The title of the book, *Preserving the Global Environment,* itself declares the totality, the whole, that is the object of concern. The specialists who deal with policy in this book are not given to talking about icons like Gaia, the earth as God's body, or the sense of the sublime that poets and others write about. On scientific grounds, they assume and establish that the issue crosses all political boundaries. They do not focus attention on the effects of my use of herbicides and pesticides in my garden, or on waste management. These smaller totalities may be of concern to the authors individually, but with their perspective on a global crisis they attend to a global analysis and, in a sense, propose global responses. There is no nostalgia for the primeval wilderness, or for a Luddite attack on technology that would in some utopian form deter, if not end, the crisis. E. F. Schumacher's proposal of some years back that small is better is not even mentioned. From their global perspective some matters that are central to the attention of many other authors are demoted in a hierarchy of importance. Yet all six "middle axioms" I quoted from Christian ethicist Nash's book are clear or implied objectives under discussion in Mathews's book.

Mathews describes the project in the following terms:

> *This volume explores part of this newly important territory that lies at the intersection of political science, economics, international law, and environmental science. Its emphasis is less on specific policies than on the processes of international governance as they relate to the management of global environmental problems. . . . There is no longer a sharp dividing line between foreign and domestic policies.*

Four causal factors of the problem are highlighted by the authors: population growth, technological economic development in general, deforestation and species loss, depletion of the ozone layer and other climate changes. If, reasonably, these are the major processes that threaten the environment globally, the response to them has to be commensurate with their causal force.

The sciences that inform the authors establish as accurately as possible *what is going on.* This is usually the first question of policy discourse, and different disciplines highlight different features. What is going on is not only a matter of scientific information but also of international economics, of political and international agreements and treaties, of political forces in both the northern and southern halves of the globe with their own national interests, etc. The problems of "justice" do come up when questions are raised as to whether certain proposals create unfair burdens on Third World countries and some other groups. But justice is not the central theme, and ethics is not one of the academic disciplines specifically included in the contributions. No Holmes Ralston appears in this book to write an essay on environmental ethics, as he does in Bormann and Kellert's *Ecology, Economics, Ethics: The Broken Circle.*

To illustrate the locus of policy discussions, some of the conclusions of the chapter on "Protecting the Ozone Layer," written by Richard Elliot Benedick, are selected. Benedick was the chief American negotiator for ozone protection treaties. He traces the developments of the Montreal Protocol for the control of the use of CFCs, the component most people know from aerosol-powered containers and air conditioners. After taking into account the most relevant factors, he suggest elements that have to be present in diplomacy— diplomacy that now deals with different issues than arms reduction, boundary negotiations, and the like.

1. "Scientists must assume an unaccustomed but critical role in international negotiations."

2. Political leaders have to take action while there are still scientific uncertainties, balancing risks and costs of action with those of not acting.

3. Education and mobilization of public opinion have to be used to generate pressure on politicians.

4. The United Nations and the American government have to provide critical leadership to mobilize international consensus.

5. It is desirable for a leading country or group of countries to take preemptive environmental action before there is global agreement.

6. Environmental organizations and industry have to participate.

7. Regulations work best when realistic market incentives are present to encourage technological innovation.

8. Economic and structural inequalities among countries have to be reflected in regulations; that is, rich countries that are responsible for the ozone-layer problem have to help poor countries implement environmental policies without sacrifices of the poor countries' hope for improved standards of living.

9. While each country's regulatory strategies can differ, the economic effects should be equivalent.

10. The signing of a treaty is not the most decisive event; the negotiations lay the proper foundations and establish working relations.

11. A treaty should not cement a status quo, but like the Montreal Protocol be designed as a dynamic and flexible instrument for an on-going process as new technical, economic, political, and other developments occur.

(There are parallels between some of these eleven conclusions and principles that have been involved negotiations for arms reductions. And, interestingly, some of the authors of essays were formerly noted for their work on arms control. Inferences that could be drawn from this observation go beyond the purposes of these chapters.)

These eleven elements note the political and economic realism of diplomacy. They answer the questions, "What is going on?" and "What is possible?" They arise out of experience in negotiations, and thus there is a narrative, a history, which informs them. To be sure, there is an overarching value preference; the global environment must be preserved for many different reasons. But negotiation is the art of finding solutions with which no party is fully satisfied and proposing alternatives that might be more satisfactory to the various interests involved. The Montreal Protocol on CFCs resulted from such a process.

An implied notion of justice functions in the eleven elements I listed; the costs, or pains, are to be as evenly distributed as possible, and the more powerful nations are to be especially concerned about the aspirations of the poor nations. But, interestingly, the concept of justice—as this is developed in the discipline of ethics—is not used. The policymaker in this case does not begin with justice, but moves from his concerns to a notion of it as a *consideration,* that is, a general concern for fairness. He gets to a kind of moral "ought," from his analysis of what is possible. The ethicist might begin with a concept of distributive justice, or of fairness, and move from it to implications for policy. Or she might, as my philosopher in the nuclear deter-

128

rence seminar, simply stay within the realm of ethical argumentation.

Mathews's book is an example of one kind of moral discourse, or morally relevant discourse if a more stringent interpretation of the moral is preferred. It is policy discourse. Nash's book is an example of another kind—in a narrower sense, ethical discourse. The contrast is clear. In Mathews the primary language, analyses, information, and concepts are from policy disciplines. What is going on and what is possible set the parameters; the moral question, justice, emerges as one consideration. In Nash and in other literature on ecological ethics, much of which has a different focus than his Christian one, the first question is "What ought to be done?" and ethical terms of varying sorts, depending upon the perspective of the author, determine the parameters; the ethical has to be applied to proposals for practice and policy, and, one hopes, determine them. It is manifestly difficult to close the circle between these two types of discourse to the satisfaction of the experts in each, or to the interests that each represents and values.

Another type of moral discourse has been alluded to in previous chapters is prophetic discourse. Bill McKibben's *The End of Nature* has a dominantly prophetic intent and effect, comparable to Jonathan Schell's *The*

Fate of the Earth, which provided an apocalyptic vision of the effects of a nuclear war and thus raised the consciousness of its dangers for many readers. There are many prophetic voices in the environmental movement; they use print and pictures. Some are strident; one thinks of Edward Abbey's anger and the more radical proposals that come from it. Wendell Berry's poetry, essays, and other writings are different from Abbey's; they lure the reader more than anger him or her.

A full-page advertisement in *The New York Times,* February 17, 1993, sponsored by David R. Brower, proclaims that "Economics is a form of brain damage." It attacks economic advisors who, it charges, ignore "what their advice to government and corporations has cost the Earth and the future." They continue to advise that "we trash the Earth." The ad uses the symbol of a clock coming close to the midnight hour that was so effective in *The Bulletin of Atomic Scientists,* beginning with a Monday at 12:01 when the earth begins, moving to 1/200 second to midnight on Saturday when the atomic age began, and ending with midnight on Saturday when "gridlock prevails." Interestingly, Sunday is left out! Brower and other environmental prophets, even the gentler among them, use Hans Jonas's "heuristics of fear" to evoke anxiety and dread because of the evils that threaten whatever we value in nature and the reasons we value it, including human survival. The prophet indicts, either by vivid portrayal of future destruction or by visions of a more edenic past of wilderness. Impatience is characteristic of the rhetoric, whether addressed to threats to beauty, biodiversity, or human survival. Apocalyptic and other prophetic discourse arouses emotions and often locates one or two primary demons (economists in the ad referred to above) that threaten the good to be preserved. Other demons are rampant consumerism, private exploitation of public lands for corporate profits, population growth, and the use of governmental authority to build huge dams, for example, on the Colorado River, destroying prehistoric natural beauty.

When prophetic voices use the more technical language of ethics (the rights of nature, or eco-justice) in addition to narratives and pictures, these bolster a deeply affective sense of crisis. Some follow through to the murkier issues of policy discourse, but others see that as dangerous incrementalism and compromise based upon special interests. But prophetic discourse does what ethical arguments and policy discourse seldom do; it raises our consciousness about the environmental crisis. Aldo Leopold, Rachel Carson, Edward Abbey, Bill McKibben, and others use evidence, rhetoric, and imagination to provoke concern to motivate various forms of action. They perceive and describe the *malum;* they provoke the "revulsion of feelings" that backs the gaining of knowledge and forwards actions.

Another type of moral discourse is narrative. It usually has a prophetic effect. One only needs to recall the "story" of the spotted owl, or of residential communities that had to be vacated because of the effects of pollution, like Love Canal, the nature films about the depletion of the rain forests in the Amazon Basin, the accounts of the wandering barge of waste that place after place refused to accept, the effects of air pollution on Central and Northern European forests, and many more. These narratives have multiple outcomes on many readers and viewers: they depict the *malum* graphically and arouse feelings of revulsion; they carry information in nonabstract, nonstatistical forms; they evoke an identification of persons with the pain and loss of other persons and other biota. The good that is to be preserved is not simply, however, the obverse side of the evil that is perceived; it is hard to develop social, economic, political, and natural utopias in which all that is threatened would flourish without compromise of cherished human benefits.

Thus, there are other stories that have different effects. Roderick Nash in *Wilderness and the American Mind* reminds us how deep in the American narrative

132

are the accounts of pioneers moving into the wilderness, heroically clearing the forests for agriculture, withstanding the perils of depression of mind and economy because of the susceptibility to the vicissitudes of nature (one is reminded, for example, of Ole Rolvaag's *Giants in the Earth* with its powerful account of settlers on the Dakota prairies), daring the perils of the Oregon, Mormon, and Santa Fe trails to "open" the West. Nature, if not the enemy, is often not the friend of humans; the stories of how it was brought under some control, cultivated, mined, and cut down for the sake of raising human living standards is also an alluring story, though not one as heartily cheered now as it was in my youth.

Into our own interpretations of the place of humans in the natural environment we take stories from non-European cultural sources. The accounts of Native Americans, both the devastating effects on their ways of life that intrusions have caused and of their religious beliefs and outlooks, are a case in point. Like my Thai monk's view, these stories recognize dependence on nature and interdependence with it as necessary for a valid way of life; an outlook of cooperation with nature is a way to find something like he sees in the law of nature, the *dhamma*. The outlook of Asian religions has surely affected American and European attitudes

133

toward nature. Many environmentalists are deeply influenced by Asian spiritualities, with their narratives, symbols, myths, and practices. The American Buddhist theologian and leader, Ronald Nakasone, in his *The Ethics of Enlightenment,* leads his reader into more general considerations through a story about Gautama's birth and life, and then relates a classic Buddhist myth. This is one's access to such a general statement as, "The fundamental aspect of the doctrine of interdependence describes the cooperative and mutually supportive relationship among all existences. . . . [C]ause and effect are not sequential, but simultaneous." Nakasone does not begin with metaphysics; his path to abstraction is through narrative.

The narratives one finds compelling are affected by, and in turn affect, one's attitude and activities. But narratives do not resolve the policy choices that are the subject of Mathews's book, nor are they ethical arguments like Nash's book or arguments for the rights of nature. One notes that a historical narrative informs policy issues, for example, how the negotiations for the Law of the Sea were conducted; it helps one know what is going on and what seems to be possible or impossible under existing legal, economic, and political conditions. But narrative does not resolve the conflicts of ends that policy choices face.

134

We have seen, in this chapter, how different academic disciplines address issues of what actions and policies are appropriate for humans in relation to the natural environment. That gap between ethical and policy discourse, introduced at the beginning, is no easier to close in environmental matters than it was in discussion of the ethics of nuclear deterrence. In Mathews's book even academic disciplines relevant to international policy are not readily convertible into common terms without significant remainders. Prophetic and narrative discourse also each contribute to our understanding, affective responses, attitudes, and outlooks, without adequately resolving all particular choices about personal conduct or about policy.

From a theocentric perspective the difficulties in closing the disciplinary arcs of the circle are no surprise. Interdependence does not automatically issue in harmony of desired and desirable ends; the multidimensionality of values, human and others, is the basis for relational values and for tensions between them. Human finitude, both knowledge and power to control all future outcomes of our actions, limits our capacities.

I often quote Milton, from *Paradise Lost,* Book 4, to make the theocentric point: "So little knows / Any, but God alone, to value right / the good before him. . . ." It remains for the concluding "coda" to address further the contributions and problems of various arcs of the circle that ideally we would like to close, and some proposals about what more satisfactory, but never complete, efforts at closure can take place.

References and Bibliographical Notes

Ecology, Economics, Ethics (New Haven: Yale University Press, 1991) was edited by F. Herbert Bormann and Stephen R. Kellert. For a fascinating study of how the circle got almost closed in one location, see J. Ronald Engel, *Sacred Sands: The Struggle for Community in the Indiana Dunes* (Middletown: Conn.: Wesleyan University Press, 1985). Engel's work is richly multidimensional, weaving everything from symbols of sacrality to economics and political lobbying and laws. One could rework the text as an account of how values of beings in various relations conflicted and were thwarted or facilitated over an important period of regional history. The most complex and successful effort that I know to propose how the circle should be closed is Herman E. Daly and John B. Cobb, Jr., *For the Common Good,* cited in the bibliographical notes for chapter 1. Laurence H. Tribe, Corinne S. Schelling, and John Voss, eds., *When Values Conflict: Essays on Environmental Analysis, Discourse and Decision* (Cambridge: Ballinger Publishing Co., 1976), a study done under the auspices of the American Academy of Arts and Sciences, is worthy of continued attention parallel to Ronald Engel's book. The quotations from James A. Nash, *Loving Nature:*

Ecological Integrity and Christian Responsibility (Nashville: Abingdon Press, 1991), are from pages 197, 203, 206, 210, 215, and 217. Jessica Tuchman Mathews, ed., *Preserving the Global Environment: The Challenge of Shared Leadership* (New York: W. W. Norton and Co., 1991), is the product of a study sponsored by Columbia University's American Assembly and the World Resources Institute from Washington, D.C.; Mathews's description of the project is from page 26. E. F. Schumacher, *Small Is Beautiful* (New York: Harper and Row, 1973), has been widely used to support forms of "appropriate technology"; for example, I heard it cited many times in India in 1978. The quotations and paraphrases from Benedick's chapter, "Protecting the Ozone Layer" can be found on pages 143–49, in a section headed "Lessons for a New Global Diplomacy." *The New Yorker Magazine* published the first versions of both McKibben's *The End of Nature* and Schell's *The Fate of the Earth* (New York: Avon Books, 1982). In addition to Wendell Berry and Edward Abbey, many other authors inform and shape the attitudes and outlooks of many people. This literature is in an American tradition, much of it brought into Roderick Nash's *Wilderness and the American Mind*. My youngest daughter had read Rolvaag's *Giants in the Earth* (New York: Harper Torch Books, 1964) before we drove across the northern prairies in the summer of 1974; her recall of its characters and their tribulations in the "pioneer days" evoked an experience of dread as we drove through hundreds of miles of open spaces. The quotation is from page 44 of Ronald Nakasone, *The Ethics of Enlightenment* (Fremont: Dharma Cloud Publishers, 1990). I have developed the variety of forms of moral discourse used here in *Varieties of Moral*

Discourse: Prophetic, Narrative, Ethical, and Policy in the Stob Lectures (Grand Rapids: Calvin College and Seminary, 1988), and with reference to medical matters in "Moral Discourse about Medicine: A Variety of Forms," *The Journal of Medicine and Philosophy* 15 (1990): 125–42.

5

Coda

We would like to close the circle of disciplines, types of moral discourse, different religious and moral outlooks, interests that have justification, none of which is convertible into the others without remainder, in order to have a firm basis for our personal and familial choices, economic choices in the private sector, political and legislative choices at every level of government, and international policy choices. But maybe what we have learned is that the circle is not the most appropriate geometrical form to use as a simile for what we desire. There might be too many arcs and, as shaped, they do not fit into a perfect circumference. They certainly cannot all fit into the perfect circle form we desire.

When we reflect on the natural environment from a theocentric perspective and think about the moral stance, the multidimensionality of values of nature in various relations, the academic disciplines that inform our choices, and the variety of moral discourse, we may have something more like a fractal than a circle. Maybe we start with a simple equilateral triangle, the points being our moral stance, information about the natural environment and our participation in it, and the disciplines of ethics and the policy sciences. But in the middle third of each line we can add another equilateral triangle, with the six-point Star of David now, and continue the procedure. Each new triangle might represent an additional complexity, built on what was simpler. But even a fractal turns out more symmetrical than the environment and our relations to it are and ought to be.

Whatever "shape" we think in, or maybe we think in musical or other symbols, at the point of a choice we necessarily close off options, shunt off various matters that have informed us, and order our responses and actions from some center of gravity and toward some end in view that seems to bring focus to our relations and our actions. To be sure, we might slothfully fail to make choices and to exert influence through our actions, letting the determining forces of nature, technology and other aspects of culture, and institutional powers in corporations and governments shape the near and distant future. Or we might self-consciously forbear, judging that we are relatively powerless, inadequately informed, and thus rely upon the judgments and actions of those who have access to power and apparent expertise.

Or we might target a particular point of the intersection of modern industrial technology and nature where we can exert some influence in full knowledge that this intersection is only one that needs attention, and that its impact might be more symbolic than efficacious in the long run. Thus we can follow Bill McKibben's poster to guide our celebration of Christmas, knowing that the outcome would not solve the tensions in negotiations about the Law of the Sea. Our question might be, "What can one person, or family, do?" and do that we will. Consumption practices, recycling, careful gardening, and other things may be small in overall impact, but collectively achieve larger desirable outcomes and rightly assuage our feelings, at least to some extent, of revulsion from the *malum* we perceive. It might be like sending a check to CARE or Church World Service to feed refugees; the deeper causes of suffering are not stemmed but there is some relief and incentive for those with more power than we have to get at deeper causes of the symptom of malnutrition and starvation.

Or, the particular point we target might be deter-

mined by our analysis of the evils that most effi-
caciously cause threats to the natural environment, including humanity as a part of it, over an extended
future time. A citation from an agricultural economist
might catch our attention. While at present we have
agricultural surpluses, and while science and technology will continue to contribute various forms of food
production, with present rates of population growth in
three decades a Malthusian crunch might occur in
many countries. Perhaps, in light of this, one might
choose to send one's money to support Zero-Population
Growth, or some other agency that is effectively seeking to reduce the rate of increase. But taking account of
economic, political, cultural, and other factors that
affect the success of such a thrust in our and other very
different parts of the world, including the charge of
First World imperialism in a new form, adds either a lot
of different shaped arcs that cannot make a circle or a
lot more triangles to the fractal.

The particular point we target might be pollution;
the various courses of action to restrain this evil cannot
all be pursued at the same time. Internationally, we
might support enforcement of the Law of the Sea, or
the Montreal Protocol; locally, we might support what
we judge to be the best waste-disposal program; personally, we might change the fertilizers we use in our gar-

den or on our crops. The range of possible courses of action and our judgment about which would be most effective will influence which of the organizations we will contribute to among the many that have our addresses on their mailing lists or annually ring our doorbells. For example, we might agree with general objectives of Greenpeace, but favor another organization's means to achieve them because we have some moral scruples about means that are used.

The moment of closure comes when we shift from being observers and analysts to being agents or actors: when we make personal and familial choices about consumption habits after learning about various problems of energy usage or waste management; when negotiators of international environmental pacts and laws finally agree on the best possible compromises of various interests, including moral and value interests; when we are deeply persuaded by information and analysis that one intersection between nature and human activity has led to a process of irreversibility that is detrimental to some aspect of life that we have reasons to cherish or to save—the snail darter, the spotted owl, or the elephant.

Intentional actions, whether forbearances or interventions into the natural environment, necessarily require some descriptive, analytical explanatory, and evaluative account of the circumstances that provoke our response. We locate the perceived *malum,* and we have to arrive at some understanding of it; where we locate it and what interpretation of it we find satisfactory largely set the parameters within which we will find effective courses of action, that is, effective forms of power to have an impact on the course of events. In the previous chapters I have noted a number of locations of the perceived *malum.* Differences between persons and groups with reference to human responsibility for the natural environment occur depending on their assessment of several things. And part of the frustration many persons have is due to the multidimensionality of values of various items in relation to other items of some extended list of concerns, causal factors, and desirable outcomes. We see at least partial correctness in various diagnoses and various proposals for action. This accounts for the growth industry of ecological ethics and ecological policy writings, to which the present book only adds.

Gibson Winter, for example, very perceptively focuses on symbols we use to interpret and understand our relation to nature and how they affect our basic attitudes and stances. He distinguishes between mechanistic and artistic ones and develops the radically altering effects of the artistic for our self-understanding and our relations with the natural environment. The proposal is for a change in theology, which like other human and moral sciences "is an ideological expression of proposals for personal fulfillment in the context of universal fulfillment." The task of "religious social ethics is essentially a critique and proposal of ideology." From the standpoint of a hermeneutic of suspicion the prevailing ideology is deconstructed to disclose the interests that sustain it and the social realities that conceal it. Thus he proposes a substitution of artistic symbols for the mechanistic ones that have dominated modern culture.

Winter's analysis, like others that use different terms, locates the root of the problem in a dominant cultural consciousness and ideology. That location requires an interpretation of what factors developed and sustained that ideology; Winter shows us how symbols do that. The call, in effect, is for a new ideology, requiring new symbols, that will better serve "personal fulfillment in the context of universal fulfillment." Winter's work is profoundly prophetic; it gets to one of the, if not *the*, root factor in the larger problem addressed in different ways by others. It is a call to radical cultural conversion. Perhaps the contributors to *Preserving the Global Environment*, edited by Jessica Tuchman Mathews, would find it hard to accomplish; their large problem is the same as Winter's, namely the crisis of global environment, but their analysis has a different focus, and thus their remedies are different.

My main point in this "coda" is that to be an intentional agent requires closure of the relevant considerations, but premature closure leads to oversimplification and possibly to excessively limited courses of action—perhaps even to imprudent ones. The policy considerations of the Mathews volume do not address the ideological issues that Winter and others address; they are not informed by hermeneutics of suspicion and show no interest in how cultural symbols shape ethos or how ethos affects choices. To Winter, in effect, the policy essays are already in a tunnel and think incrementally about how to find light at its end; his approach implies that it is the wrong tunnel, or at least that there ought to be more than one. Ethical arguments, whether those of James A. Nash and other Christian writers or proponents of the rights of nature, call attention to moral aspects of different courses of action in various spheres, and provide action guides. The same gulf I illustrated from Robert Sachs's and my effort to bring various disciplines to bear on the ethics of nuclear deterrence faces the legislators, international negotiators, and even individual persons when tensions emerge among desirable ends for our participation in the natural environment.

Conscientious choices of action, whether about how I tend my garden, how to further develop the Montreal Protocol, or how the legislatures of Oregon or the United States ought to relate economic ends to conservation ends, ought to be as thoroughly informed as possible. This necessitates as critical an understanding of the sources of information as agents can grasp, since the sources, whether they are ecological interest groups or corporations, can select evidences to fit canons of proof so that a reader or hearer is persuaded.

Conscientious choices of action ought to have their ends in view, so that the desired outcomes are as reasonably achievable as the means appropriate to them. This has to be done in recognition that the end in view is never comprehensive and that other particular ends ought also to be approximated or achieved. My scrupulosity about what pesticides and herbicides I use is not sufficient to achieve what the essays in Mathews's book seek to achieve, but their end implies that I restrain my use of chemicals in my garden, though they do not propose it.

Conscientious choices ought to be capable of action, that is, they ought to occur from the basis of whatever capacities and powers are available to agents. Different social roles carry different opportunities and responsibilities; an amateur gardener has a different basis for affecting outcomes than a lobbyist or legislator. Capacities and powers, however, are not limited to who we are and where we happen to be; relevant ones can be developed by joining in common interest with others. We see this all around us. Perhaps the perception of an environmental crisis has spawned more new voluntary associations and strengthened more old ones than any other issue in recent decades. It is premature to close the knowledge and insight of our sources before we have explored new sources of capacities and powers to act. Agents are not limited to access to one form of power or capacities.

Humans are to seek to discern what God is enabling and requiring them to be and to do as participants in the patterns and processes of interdependence of life in the world. The divine ordering is perceived, insofar as it is humanly possible, in and through the ordering of nature, culture, history, and personal living. It has no equilibrium which guarantees the realization of all justifiable ends, and our ends as developers of technology and culture infinitely complicate the achievement of even a dynamic one. We are to relate all things to each other in ways that concur with their relations to God, again, insofar as this can be discerned. But God will be God. As intentional participants we have responsibility, and the destiny of the natural environment and our parts in it is heavily in our hands, but the ultimate destiny of all that exists is beyond our human control.

Reference

The quotations are from Winter, *Liberating Creation: Foundations of Religious Social Ethics* (New York: Crossroad Publishing Co., 1981), 128 and 129.

Appendix A

Response to the 1992 Moll Lectures by James Gustafson

Michael Melampy

Associate Professor of Biology
Baldwin-Wallace College

The opportunity to respond to the 1992 Moll Lectures by James Gustafson represents a special honor for a me as a biologist. It allows me to continue a long tradition of discourse between biologists and theologians. Explanations of the origins, distribution, and behavior of different life forms have borrowed from both scientific and theological constructs over the millennia. Charles Darwin is an excellent example of this tradition. Darwin was a theology student at Cambridge before making his famous voyage on the *Beagle,* and his background in theology, particularly his reading of the English natural theologian William Paley, certainly had an influence on his biology. As Gustafson richly demonstrates, theology and biology continue to intersect in many important ways, and it is appropriate and necessary that we explore these intersections, especially as they relate to environmental issues.

Gustafson has described nature as being characterized by conflict or dissonance, as a set of interdependent relationships characterized by tension and disequilibrium. This vision of nature is very insightful in that it recognizes both the creative and destructive impact of unpredictable disturbances. Natural interrelationships constantly change as the result of disturbances that alter physical conditions and impose new limits to population growth. Much of the biotic diversity that we associate with natural ecosystems would quickly disappear without disturbances that provide the conditions upon which opportunistic organisms depend. This is a fact that has only slowly been accepted within the scientific community, and it is gratifying to see it gain credence among theologians.

Disequilibrium due to disturbance makes nature resistant to simple cause-and-effect analysis. Natural causes and effects are contingent upon prevailing physical and biological properties that may change due to unforeseen disturbances. Disturbance on a small scale, such as a treefall creating a gap of intense light in an otherwise dark forest understory, may increase the diversity of local conditions and allow for the coexistence of more species. Large scale disturbances, such as a meteor striking the earth or global warming due to the greenhouse effect, are more likely to reduce the number of pieces in the environmental mosaic and make it impossible for some organisms to persist.

The great challenge that we as humans face is the need to restrain our activities and avoid producing the large-scale disturbances that reduce natural diversity. Humans, with their incredible mental dexterity, have an unprecedented ability to alter nature in order to achieve specific goals. If those goals are defined only in terms of short-term gratification, then we will continue to alter or disturb nature so as to extract the resources we require to support more humans and more human consumption. If we cannot restrain our activities, then it is likely that environmental degradation will continue until our own existence is seriously jeopardized.

Gustafson offers no simple mechanisms for achieving human restraint. Instead, he suggests that we begin to seek restraint by "ordering nature." This ordering would presumably involve an attempt to allocate natural resources among the biotic components of nature in a way that protects natural diversity and the interrelationships upon which we depend. Of course, any intelligent ordering must rely on scientific facts concerning the relative importance of different natural interrelationships. As we gather more knowledge about nature, we must constantly adjust our ordering. This will require a tremendous commitment to the study of nature and to the interpretation of the results of our studies. So far, I see little evidence of that commitment. We have scarcely started even to catalog many of the components of nature, especially such small creatures as insects.

Gustafson intimates that human commitment to the protection of nature can arise from a sense of ethical obligation, which may be derived from religious traditions. I am not in a position to evaluate the efficacy of religious traditions in generating a sense of ethics; in my view, religious traditions have generated both ethical and unethical behavior. However, I do agree that a sense of ethical obligation is needed. The development of this sense will depend on the degree to which humans understand their dependence on nature. Our dependence can and is being demonstrated in a very rational manner by scientists and teachers. But a sense of ethical obligation will also require an emotional attachment to nature, the type of attachment that will cause a real sense of loss when parts of nature are destroyed. I maintain that we are losing our emotional attachment to nature. As we live in an increasingly urban and artificial environment, we are losing touch with most of the biotic components of nature. As we lose familiarity, we lose our sense of the majesty and wonder of nature. Instead, feelings of fear and revulsion may be evoked upon encountering an insect that is a perfectly good example of the intricate adaptations and interrelationships so common in nature. The real saviors of nature and the human species may be those individuals who take the time to introduce children to the wonder of nature and nurture an emotional attachment between children and insects.

Appendix B

Response to James M. Gustafson

David Krueger

Spahr Professor of Managerial and Corporate Ethics
Baldwin-Wallace College

This brief treatise embodies well the rich scope of qualities and ingredients that have characterized James Gustafson's writings for so many decades. Its substantive foundation is theocentric ethics. It brings conceptual order out of the complex and multifaceted terrain of theological ethics by providing typological road maps that permit us to compare and contrast theological and ethical positions that span the broad scope of the field. This he accomplishes with the clarity of thought and language that has long been Gustafson's refreshing trademark within a field that often seems to measure the quality and social contribution of its scholarship in inverse relation to its intelligibility to those outside its field and to the wider public. It demonstrates the commitment to careful, rigorous, crossdisciplinary conversation that is essential to theological ethical inquiry, especially of a topic so vast as the environment. It embodies humility in its arguments, conclusions, and prescriptions, based on the author's recognition of the sheer vastness of the subject matter, his ubiquitous recognition of pluralism, and thus his abiding appreciation for the integrity of alternative positions and conclusions, but also more deeply founded on basic theological and epistemological affirmations that assert the limits to human knowledge. Finally, it is richly autobiographical; it opens the reader not only to the deeply personal ways in which the author's life experiences and history inform his own theocentric ethic of nature, but also to the important affective roles that reverence, wonder, and awe play in shaping his outlook on the world.

I will attempt two things in this response. First, I will highlight in summary fashion some of Professor Gustafson's most important claims in these lectures, in an attempt to show how he thinks theocentric ethics might construct an environmental ethic. Second, I will consider whether or not the structure and logic of his theocentric ethic might permit us to draw broader and more general predictive and prescriptive conclusions about the destiny of our planet.

I will attempt very briefly to highlight and reflect upon some of the ways that Gustafson understands theological ethics to reflect upon the environment and indeed, more specifically, how he understands a theocentric perspective might shape an environmental ethic.

Gustafson clearly demonstrates that theology and ethics are not monolithic. Rather, there is a rich variety of ways to think theologically and ethically about the environment, within Christianity, Western culture, and beyond. Much of the beauty and value of Gustafson's work is its ability to provide us with clear conceptual road maps to organize our thought, such as typologies of positions with respect to the environment. For the question "Why should we be concerned with nature?" he provides a typology of fundamental philosophical orientations ranging from purely intrinsic to purely instrumental. For the question "How should humans relate to nature?" he provides a typology of moral stances ranging from despotism to subordination. In considering how Christians might make ethical judgments about the environment, he offers his four-part road map of modes of moral discourse—prophetic, narrative, ethical, and policy discourse.

In his conclusion, Gustafson summarizes the fundamental theocentric perspective as developed in *Ethics from a Theocentric Perspective* that organizes his ethical reflection on the environment:

> *Humans are to seek to discern what God is enabling and requiring them to be and to do as participants in the patterns and processes of interdependence of life in the world. . . . It has no equilibrium which guarantees the realization of all justifiable ends, and our ends as developers of technology and culture infinitely complicates the achievement of even a dynamic one. We are to relate all things to each other in ways that concur with their relations to God, again, insofar as this can be discerned. But God will be God. As intentional participants we have responsibility, and the destiny of the natural environment and our parts in it is heavily in our hands, but the ultimate destiny of all that exists is beyond our human control.*

This theocentric perspective utilizes the knowledge of human experience ("observations about all life in the world") and modern sciences to discern the fact that God is the power that creates and sustains life, as well as bears down, limits, threatens, and destroys it. We depend upon the interdependent patterns and processes of life, yet they result in no single discernable or ideal harmony, at least not harmonies that are necessarily good for humans. For some, this experience is interpreted as a sense of the divine in nature. This theological posture coheres with or implies a moral stance of human participation in nature. As such, humans are authorized to intervene in nature for the sake of humans as well as nature, but ultimately with no sufficient or comprehensive knowledge of "the good," certainly not in the way that a Thomist would claim to know. At best, a theocentric stance permits us to discern "a dynamism of interdependencies that warns us of limitations and awakens us to threats to human well-being as well as to the biodiversity of life itself." While we are duty-bound to seek to discern how the parts, of which we are one, function in relation to the whole of nature, and while we must inevitably, but always tentatively, assign values to those parts, we can never do so definitively. "There is not a harmony." "It is not ours to know such things." Inexorable conflicts of values are a fundamental aspect of the "order" of nature. A theocentric ethic can provide parameters and tentative directives, but perhaps never definitive conclusions or prescriptions. Minimally, Gustafson claims that the following imperative can guide us, "Act so that you consider all things never *only* as a means to your ends, or even to collective human ends." Nature has intrinsic value; the good of humanity may not reside at the apex of creation.

Might we not go further, though, and infer an even stronger general moral imperative consistent with a theocentric perspective that affirms the moral stance of participation in nature: "Act in ways that minimize human disruptions to the dynamic equilibria of nature. Aim to preserve and extend as far into the future as possible the dynamic flourishing and destruction of life (biodiversity) on our planet."

This latter moral imperative would imply and depend upon a more substantive vision of the good (*bonum*), perhaps more substantive than Gustafson would feel comfortable in asserting. Just how much order can we discern from the dynamic and changing equilibria of the natural world? This question leads me to my concluding query about a theocentric environmental ethic: Can the structure and logic of Gustafson's theocentric ethic permit us to draw broader and more general inferences and conclusions about the environmental destiny of our planet? Do the evidences of human experience and the human sciences with respect to nature tend toward ambiguity or clarity? Are the patterns and effects of human intervention with nature aiming us and/or nature toward destruction or not? Or, finally, are these things not for us to know?

One imagines Gustafson would hesitate and wish to resist the temptation to make such a broad predictive generalization. If he were to hazard one, it would be carefully and cautiously qualified. Indeed, Gustafson has never been prone to prophetic, doomsday moral conclusions and prescriptions. Yet he does utilize the language of crisis in this treatise. "[W]hat had always been a disturbance about the state of the natural environment has now become a global crisis. Naming it a global crisis now affects our perceptions and our stances." He acknowledges that what is perhaps distinctive and new about the global context within which we must construct environmental ethics today is the sense of crisis—the affective revulsion of feeling which acts ahead of knowledge when confronted with the immensity of the threats (*malum*) to human life and to nature itself. Are we not perceiving the threat of an evil outcome on a global scale to an extent never before felt and known? Does this not explain the new wave of environmentalism: "ugliness is repulsive to us; in turn, we value the threatened beauty of the natural world"? Yes, indeed, for we all are practically engaged in what Hans Jonas describes as a perception of the evil and revulsion against it *as the first order of thought and action.*

What can we say constructively about a theocentric

environmental ethic? It will not provide us with a complete blueprint for human policies and choices. Rather, ambiguity and uncertainty are inherent aspects of the enterprise. We cannot read off of nature precisely what our human activity ought always to be, but we must use the patterns and processes of interdependence as *one basis* for our moral conduct. Not to do so invites perilous outcomes, for humans or for biodiversity. We need constantly to define restraints on human action; for example, if CFCs contribute to the depletion of the ozone layer, we should radically restrain, if not eliminate, our use of them. Our policy responses must be global, collaborative, multidisciplinary and multisectoral—aiming at the preservation of nature's dynamic equilibria, as well as we can partially glimpse them.

What would Gustafson say that we can infer and predict about the long-term prospects for our planet and for human and nonhuman life forms? The evidences of human experience and the human sciences seem mixed.

On the one side, one can see such hopeful developments and trends as the following:

- a growing environmental consciousness within the West;

- increased descriptive scientific knowledge of how our human actions negatively affect aspects of nature, even on a global scale;

- global, collaborative efforts such as the United Nations-sponsored 1992 Rio Environmental Summit, which examined the world's most pressing environmental challenges, as well as problem-specific success stories such as the Montreal Protocol, whose intended outcome is the complete cessation of production of CFCs;

- steady incremental progress in government regulations and market adjustments that are accounting more fully for the environmental costs and benefits of human actions.

Are we turning the corner? Do these trends provide reason for hope, which Gustafson defines as "the conditions of possibility for preserving and enhancing what we can justifiably value"? Or, is there much greater presumption in favor of pessimism, consistent with the notion of crisis? For illustrative evidence here I would cite:

- global human population growth that will most likely double within the next century from five billion to ten billion people—perhaps challenging the very carrying capacity of the earth itself;

- increased forms of environmental degradation such as global warming and deforestation of rain forests;

- continually increasing rates of depletion of non-renewable energy sources, most notably fossil fuels.

These latter trends support the argument of crisis. Can we sort through the ambiguities and ambivalences of the evidence about nature and human intervention in nature to hazard a predictive generalization one way or the other? If so, and if we embrace the argument of environmental crisis, then it would seem that a theo-centric environmental ethic might support and indeed require environmental policies and prescriptions of a fairly radical bent, moving beyond the incremental pace of change that seems to be a constitutive feature of modern society.

Yet, if the argument of crisis is sustainable and if these negative trends of human intervention in nature cannot be sufficiently reversed, then the theocentric ethicist might conclude that our destiny, indeed our fate, as humans and as a planet, is all but certain. Life as we know it will come to an end. What harmonies and equilibria we discern and experience eventually will disappear to be replaced by disharmonies and disequilibria, at least with respect to the good of the human species. While our moral imperative might be to extend the life of the planet, including our own species, as long as possible, we must finally acknowledge that we are finite and mortal. God is God; planetary life, while created good by God, will surely die. God be praised.

Index

173